How To Stress Less

Simple ways to stop worrying and take control of your future

Benjamin Bonetti

CAPSTONE
A Wiley Brand

This edition first published 2014 © Benjamin Bonetti

Registered office
John Wiley and Sons Ltd, The Atrium, Southern Gate, Chichester, West Sussex, PO19 8SQ, UK

For details of our global editorial offices, for customer services and for information about how to apply for permission to reuse the copyright material in this book please see our website at www.wiley.com.

Wiley publishes in a variety of print and electronic formats and by print-on-demand. Some material included with standard print versions of this book may not be included in e-books or in print-on-demand. If this book refers to media such as a CD or DVD that is not included in the version you purchased, you may download this material at http://booksupport.wiley.com. For more information about Wiley products, visit www.wiley.com.

Designations used by companies to distinguish their products are often claimed as trademarks. All brand names and product names used in this book and on its cover are trade names, service marks, trademark or registered trademarks of their respective owners. The publisher and the book are not associated with any product or vendor mentioned in this book. None of the companies referenced within the book have endorsed the book.

Limit of Liability/Disclaimer of Warranty: While the publisher and author have used their best efforts in preparing this book, they make no representations or warranties with the respect to the accuracy or completeness of the contents of this book and specifically disclaim any implied warranties of merchantability or fitness for a particular purpose. It is sold on the understanding that the publisher is not engaged in rendering professional services and neither the publisher nor the author shall be liable for damages arising herefrom. If professional advice or other expert assistance is required, the services of a competent professional should be sought.

Library of Congress Cataloging-in-Publication Data

Bonetti, Benjamin, 1982-
  How to stress less : simple ways to stop worrying and take control of your future / Benjamin Bonetti.
      pages cm
  Includes index.
  ISBN 978-0-85708-468-2 (paperback)
  1. Stress management. 2. Stress (Psychology) I. Title.
  RA785.B652 2014
  155.9'042 – dc 3

                                            2014007534

A catalogue record for this book is available from the British Library.

ISBN 978-0-857-08468-2 (paperback)
ISBN 978-0-857-08465-1 (ebk) ISBN 978-0-857-08466-8 (ebk)

Cover design by Dan Jubb
Set in 11/14.5pt SabonLTStd-Roman by Laserwords Private Limited, Chennai, India.
Printed in Great Britain by TJ International Ltd, Padstow, Cornwall, UK

This book is dedicated to the following:

Amy Levin
Victoria Zoutewelle
L.P

CONTENTS

INTRODUCTION

We know what stress does but we do not know what stress is!

It's always best to start at the very beginning, so let's start this book by exploring the potential causes of stress; what stress is and what it is not, and how stress affects all of us. From there, we can go on to discover how to manage stress with ease and release the everyday pressures of life for good.

Throughout the book you will be asked to complete a number of tasks. Of course, these are optional, but let me just say that the more you complete, the more you will experience the overall benefits of the coaching process. The tasks are tried-and-tested tools I have used to great effect with a number of clients both directly and indirectly, and they are also used in my bestselling audios as well as in face-to-face consultations.

The following content outlines what I consider to be the three critical elements of controlling and managing stress. Note that I did not say *eliminate* stress: in my opinion stress can only be controlled not removed, but more on this later.

The three elements are:

1. Lifestyle
2. Nutrition
3. Fitness

In the coming pages, I explain the importance of creating a state of equilibrium across all three, and how each can be implemented without the need for radical changes in your current lifestyle.

Stress is a way we think, not the way we are ...

It's scientifically proven that stress, unless managed in an appropriate way, will affect all aspects of your life – essentially having an adverse effect on everything you value and care about. This makes it bigger than just the word "stress", and more complex than simply the feelings you have and the behaviours or actions that follow as a consequence of those feelings. It is a self-evolving destructive ball that unless stopped, can quickly destroy your self-worth.

It's also worth noting that stress is known to cause secondary illnesses such as weight gain/loss, anxiety, substance abuse and a whole range of other unwanted issues. Although secondary, these issues can at times take the lead role and divert to the primary position.

Coping with something isn't an option, it's a choice.

Make the choice not to cope with, put up with or accept that life has dealt you a stressful path. Choose instead to *deal with it*, and utilize your past learning to make your life one that you are truly proud to call your own.

 **Think**

What does stress mean to you?

 **Task**

Take a moment now to think about your personal definition of stress and how it manifests in your life, and then write down the behaviours you associate with being stressed.

(Continued)

How do you "do" stress?

....

....

....

....

....

....

Step One
UNDERSTANDING AND REASONING

"Things do not change; we change."

– Henry David Thoreau

Where do we start?

Self-realization is the first step towards a brighter future in every aspect of change. Knowing an issue exists and being honest about it is often the largest obstacle a person must overcome to be able to move forwards. It's the realization that life *could* be better than it currently is that becomes a key motivator to change. The pain of understanding that change is a choice, and it's a choice that wasn't taken earlier, is a fantastic trigger.

The way we feel about ourselves inwardly is projected outwardly in the way we see the world around us. If you feel grumpy and upset, the environment around you is likely to highlight only the aspects that serve to confirm your state of mind.

"We are extraordinary in the universe in that our only limits are those we place on ourselves."

Alan Bean (fourth person to walk on the moon!)

Avoid the addition of other factors ...

Stress for me is encountered when the boundaries within a certain area are being stressed. Just as the fibres on a rope become stressed when tension is applied, the same happens within our thinking and physiology. The more pressure there is, the more tension there is; the more tension, the greater the chance that there will be some form of catastrophic failure.

Having treated and educated a number of people with an adopted stress state, one thing has become very clear: these individuals all adopt a state that shows one or more of the following conditions/behaviours. Consider whether any of these match or relate to you:

- **General lethargy** – a general lack of motivation to get up in the morning, and so on.
- **Muscle tension** – a feeling of tight muscles, especially around the head and shoulders.
- **Generally unwell** – a feeling of being unwell, yet no specific symptoms to help diagnose the problem.
- **Snappy and irritable** – a tendency to get into arguments with loved ones over petty issues.
- **Lack of focus** – a lack of concentration in general, and the inability to finish even the most simplistic of tasks.
- **A sense of feeling lost** – a sense of being alone, exacerbated by a lack of motivation to socialize or spend time with friends and family.

Important note: it's perfectly normal to have any one or more of the above symptoms. Accept this and switch your focus from this point forward towards betterment, *not* procrastinating on the past state.

So what happens when your stress levels go beyond the manageable level?

If your stress levels get beyond being manageable, it's time to seek further professional advice from your local doctor or health care professional. It's my belief that the contents of this book will help you to uncover the root cause of your stress and provide you with the tools you need to resolve stress, but it's important to be aware that there are times when "stress" is not the primary issue and it can be a symptom of something much more.

Stress is nothing more than a behavioural state.

Each one of us has our own set of stress triggers. For some, getting stuck in traffic and arriving late at work triggers a stress response; for others, it takes something akin to being chased by a lion to trigger a stress response. However, the stress response is the same in all of us, irrespective of the trigger.

The stress response is a process controlled by the sympathetic nervous system, which is basically the part of your neurology that gears you up ready for a "challenging" situation. Stress is very often considered to be a modern day infliction and a result of our fast-paced modern lifestyles, but it is in fact an innate response that has been fundamentally important to the survival of mankind throughout the ages. In the days of our prehistoric ancestors, the stress response was simply a "fight-or-flight" response that prepared us to stand our ground and fight for survival in a life-threatening situation or turn tail and run for our lives! The stresses we face today in everyday life are unlikely to be matters of life and death, but the response in the human body remains the same ... our sympathetic nervous system still prepares us to fight or take flight for our very survival.

The physiological response to stress

In response to a stress trigger, a hormone called adrenaline is released from the adrenal glands. The presence of adrenaline in your blood supply then generates several physical reactions, all intended to help you survive the life-or-death crisis you're facing!

The physical reactions include:

- Sugar being released from the liver into the blood to give your body an energy boost in preparation for the fight or the run for the hills!
- An increase in your breathing rate so that you can take in more oxygen.
- An increase in your heart rate to speed up the delivery of the extra sugar and oxygen to your muscles and brain.

- An increase in your cholesterol levels to help thicken your blood and make it clot more easily should you suffer an injury.
- A slowing of your digestion processes, as the digestion of food is deemed a non-essential function in a crisis situation – your energy is needed elsewhere.

In prehistoric times, all of these physical reactions were crucial to survival when faced with situations that represented very real and immediate danger, such as being stalked by a sabre-toothed tiger. The "dangers" we face in modern life are much less immediate – chasing a looming deadline, traffic jams, or just not having enough hours in the day to tackle everything that needs to be done, for example. This means that your body is now subjected to a much more prolonged stress response. It's this prolonged exposure to the physical reactions of the stress response that's responsible for today's stress-related illnesses.

"Stress is the trash of modern life – we all generate it but if you don't dispose of it properly, it will pile up and overtake your life."

Danzae Pace

Under normal circumstances, the daily running of your body is controlled by the parasympathetic nervous system. When your senses detect that you're facing a "challenging" situation, your body switches systems and the resulting flood of essential hormones and chemicals allows you to perform at your peak when you need it most for defence/protection.

The stress hormones in brief

Adrenaline – this hormone is produced by the adrenal glands after the brain has sent a message to indicate there's an immediate "danger" or what it perceives to be a stressful situation. Its release generates the "energy rush" or "buzz" we experience as our heart pounds and breathing rate speeds up.

Noradrenaline – is a hormone similar to adrenaline but is produced by the adrenal glands and the brain. Its release, like adrenaline, generates an increase in heart rate and breathing rate and it also increases your mental alertness. The presence of noradrenaline also helps to divert the flow of blood away from non-essential functions such as digestion, so that a greater supply of oxygen can be made available to muscles and other "fight-or-flight" functions in the body.

Cortisol – this hormone is often referred to as "the stress hormone". It is also produced by the adrenal glands but its release and the effects it generates take longer to kick in than adrenaline and noradrenaline. It essentially helps to maintain essential functions in your body, such as blood pressure and fluid balance during a stressful situation, as well as regulating the non-essential functions. However, when the stress response becomes prolonged (worrying about something for a lengthy period of time, for example) cortisol continues to be produced and the effects of having too much cortisol in the body are detrimental to your health. It can lead to raised blood pressure and blood sugar levels, lowered immunity, a decreased libido, skin issues such as acne and it's also a factor in obesity.

Our innate senses will naturally protect us from danger.

In a nutshell, the stress response is designed to give us a better chance of survival when the chips are down! You could say that it gives your body temporary "superhuman" powers to boost your chances, but that's the problem right there – the response is meant to be temporary and the physical reactions are meant to be used to good and *immediate* effect.

 **Think**

Take a moment to look back at your response to the question, "How do you 'do' stress?" Consider the situations you find yourself in that trigger a stress response in your body, and think about the way it makes you feel and the way you react to it.

Now consider the following two scenarios:

One – You're walking home along a dimly lit footpath after a night out with friends when you notice a group of "suspicious" youths blocking your way up ahead. There's no escape route: you either need to keep going and hope

(Continued)

to get through, or you turn around and go back the way you came. You decide to keep going, but as you get closer to them, you feel your stress levels rise. Adrenaline surges around your body as your "fight-or-flight" response kicks in – you're ready for anything! Your heart is pounding and every one of your senses is on high alert, ready to pick up on and respond to any hint of danger. As it is, absolutely nothing happens and you pass by the youths without incident. However, you choose to use the physical reactions you're experiencing in your body to get as far away from the potential danger as you can, and you reach your home in record time!

Two – You're sitting at your desk at work and you've got a "to do" list that's the length of your arm but you're unable to get on with any of it because your mind is on other things. Later that day you've got to stand in front of a group of business directors and give a presentation that justifies your position in the company. Just the thought of having to do it is enough to get your heart pounding, and the more you think about it, the more you feel that you might be physically sick. You spend the next six hours in this state, and then you receive a message saying that your presentation has been postponed until the following afternoon. You now continue to "stress" about the situation you're in for another 24 hours.

The physical response to stress is the same in each scenario. However, in scenario one, the physical reaction is put to good use *immediately* and your body is then able to return to its normal state whereas in scenario two, the stress response is prolonged and your body is kept in this "stressed" state for a far longer period of time than nature intended.

Stress isn't just something we experience in our minds; it takes up a large amount of energy from our body, hence my linguistic alteration that we *do* stress rather than *have* stress.

Why do we have different stress thresholds?

We are all genetically different, not only physically but also emotionally, so we all respond differently to everyday happenings and events. A stressful situation for one is not necessarily stressful for another, but we all have our own thresholds beyond which the stress response will kick in. The more we build our understanding (by means of education) and improve our overall health and fitness, the more able we are to adapt to the demands of our lifestyle and to raise our stress threshold in the process.

Think about it this way: if we were armed with the knowledge to *not* stress then why would we stress in the first place?

To learn how to manage stress, it's essential to understand and accept that stress is something we *all* encounter. We all have a "built-in" stress response; managing stress is just a matter of working out a system that best suits you, allowing you to then utilize it when required.

You're not alone; and you are not the first person to "suffer" as a result of poor stress management.

Education and the consequent ability to work out your own stress strategies will not only maximize your potential to work and perform to a higher level, it will also boost your confidence to face "stressful" situations head-on and achieve what in the past may have felt *un*achievable.

Thought provoking stats on stress ...

Harvard Research – visits to the doctor are estimated to be 60 to 90 per cent due to stress-related issues and symptoms. These include chronic pain, backache, headache, asthma, allergies, insomnia, skin disorders, hypertension, diabetes, heart attack and depression, and accidents that occur as a result.

"Homeostasis" – a study of accountants in the busiest time of the tax year revealed that cholesterol levels increased significantly during this period, even when there was no significant change in diet. A study of medical students during exam time showed the same results.

British Medical Journal (2006) – statistics show that the death rate from stroke and heart attack doubled in workers facing unemployment as their workplaces downsized during the economic downturn.

Duke University Medical Center – research revealed that over 50 per cent of adults experience insomnia and have difficulty sleeping on more than three nights each week, and 25 per cent experience difficulty every night for periods of more than a month at a time.

Yale Research – a study of WWII veterans revealed that severe stress may increase the risk of stroke even many years after the initial trauma. Fifty years after the war, the incidence of stroke was eight times higher in veterans who had been prisoners of war compared to those who had not been taken prisoner.

Hebrew University – the results of research indicate that stress increases the ability of prescribed drugs to pass from the blood to the brain. Many medicines are currently produced in the assumption that the barrier between the blood and the brain, which protects it from any blood-borne toxins, can't be crossed.

Journal of the American Medical Association – studies reveal a link between negative emotions such as frustration, tension or sadness, and heart abnormalities that may cause permanent heart damage.

American Journal of Cardiology – a study concluded that stress management is as beneficial as aerobic exercise in terms of helping to prevent a major cardiac event.

Nurse Practitioner – a study involving inner-city residents with symptoms of depression, diabetes, hypertension, chronic pain, and anxiety, revealed that meditation led to a 50 per cent reduction in symptoms overall and a 70 per cent decrease in symptoms of anxiety.

Journal of Applied Psychology – a study of 22 hospitals implementing a stress prevention programme revealed a 50 per cent drop in medical errors and a 70 per cent drop in malpractice claims compared to a control group of 22 hospitals without a stress prevention programme in place.

Psychosomatic Medicine – a study of workers reporting high levels of stress and unhappiness in their jobs were trained in meditation techniques for a period of eight weeks. Brain scans prior to the training showed high levels of right-brain activity in all of the workers, indicating a negative disposition. Scans taken after the eight weeks of meditation showed an increase in left-brain activity, indicating a shift to a more positive disposition. The workers reported feeling happier and generally more enthusiastic about work and life. After the eight-week period, the workers and a control group who had not been given meditation training were given flu injections to test their immune responses. Those who meditated developed more flu virus antibodies than those who did not meditate, and higher levels of left-brain activity were also found in the group showing the stronger immune response.

University of Michigan – of 23 health concerns for children that were ranked according to a children's hospital poll, stress took the top position.

Several studies centred on workplace stress have revealed that stress-related issues are responsible for:

19 per cent of absenteeism
30 per cent of short- and long-term disability
40 per cent of employee turnover
55 per cent EAP (Employee Assistance Programmes) assistance requests
60 per cent of workplace accidents.

Step Two
OVERCOMING AND EDUCATING

"A day of worry is more exhausting than a week of work."
– John Lubbock

Along with lifestyle changes, your stress threshold will also change, so it's always important to take note of any events or situations that cause a fluctuation in your current threshold.

The fundamental elements of controlling and managing stress

1. **Lifestyle** – the way we live has a huge role to play in our reflected history and future. Stress is often referred to as something that work or employment offers: a by-product of the way we live in an effort to make a living and make a life for ourselves.

2. **Nutrition** – this is an area many other therapies or self-help concepts fail to identify, or they place very little emphasis on it. To me, nutrition is as important as all other factors in the diagnosis of stress. With poor nutrition, your body and brain fails to function effectively or at its peak potential.

3. **Fitness** – maintaining a functional level of fitness at the very least is essential in terms of ensuring every system

in your body is able to work to its full capacity with optimal efficiency.

All of these work together in harmony: if there's an imbalance in one, all of them will tumble.

The way you feel about your life is the way you will live your life, and the way you will look back on your life in years to come. Ask yourself this: would you be happy to look back at your life and know that you didn't take the action you could have taken to radically change the way you feel about your life – and therefore the way you live your life and the way you look back on it now?

There can be times in life when "stress" distorts the way we see the world and the way we feel about life. This distorted external image is something I call a "life false reading" and it's a false reading that's based largely on our internal "mood" and the associated chemical reactions going on within. However, this reading is not true in many ways ...

 **Think**

Have you ever been in a situation where prior events or happenings led to you behaving or reacting in a way that under normal circumstances would have been quite different?

The mood you are in prior to a negative event magnifies the way you see it.

Important note: You must accept that no matter how successful you are and no matter how much planning takes place, life will always offer challenges.

"I keep the telephone of my mind open to peace, harmony, health, love and abundance. Then, whenever doubt, anxiety or fear try to call me, they keep getting a busy signal – and soon they'll forget my number."

Edith Armstrong

Stress loading

Have you ever played the classic kids' game "Buckaroo"? If you have, you can use the mental image as a way of picturing the effects of stress loading. Our bodies continue to cope with ongoing incremental pressures up to a certain point but when we reach our upper limits, our capacity to cope is eventually depleted and we become unable to withstand the constant drain.

We only have so much in our reserve tank: use it all and everything fails.

Just as a car will only run a certain distance on a tank of fuel, our bodies only have a certain tolerance to stress. When the tank is drained, it needs to be replenished, and if you continue to add stress when the tank is drained, your body enters a state that I call "stress shock".

Stress shock

Stress shock should be interpreted as stress followed by shock, because it's the process of bouncing dangerously close to the limits of your stress tolerance until your reserve tank is drained and your engine effectively blows. We all have thresholds and, unfortunately, it's usually only once we've reached this level that we decide to make the much-needed change.

It is my belief that in *most* Western cultures we are reactive to pain, where as many Eastern cultures are proactive.

Being motivated by pain isn't necessarily a bad thing, but taking positive action to ensure that the level of pain isn't reached in the first place offers a much better solution and direction. You need to take positive action to manage your stress levels through lifestyle, fitness and nutrition, and combining all three categories allows you to work within a certain criteria and to create your own plan. Remember, we all experience stress in different ways and therefore we cannot work through a "one-strategy-suits-all" process.

Rest, recover and resolve

Rest, recover and resolve are three essential aspects of stress management. This is something I learnt while in the army where R&R has been used for many hundreds of years and is an essential part of military life.

R&R, military slang for rest and recuperation (or rest and relaxation) is a term used for the free time of a soldier in the US military or International UN staff serving in non-family duty stations. R&R includes various forms, including mail, sports, film screenings, using the services of leave and MWR (Morale, Welfare and Recreation).

Source: Wikipedia

By adapting the R&R concept slightly, we are able to put ourselves in a much stronger position to resolve any challenging situations that arise through being fully rested and recovered at all times. Achieving this state ensures that we keep the clarity required for clear stress planning at its peak.

 Task

Create your own stress assessment ...

A stress assessment is very much like a risk assessment. A risk assessment is used to grade the potential risks involved in doing something. For example, a sports coach must fill in a risk assessment form if he or she wishes to hold a session in a new location, especially if it's an outdoor one. The potential risks for those taking part must be noted – risks such as the potential to trip over rough ground or tree roots, or the hazard posed by having to cross a busy road to get to the location. Each risk is graded on a numerical scale with higher risks being given a higher number, and the measures that can be taken to minimize the risk in each case are also recorded. Once completed, the final score on the form is then used to make an informed decision about the suitability of the location – or in other words, whether or not it's just too risky! A risk assessment helps you to identify the risks involved in doing something and then to establish whether or not those risks are acceptable and/or manageable.

(Continued)

By using the same basic principle, you can create your own stress assessment form to help you identify potential stress triggers and give them a numerical grade according to the stress load they represent. The higher your final score becomes, the closer to a state of stress shock you become, so you can effectively use your score as a way of making a choice – the choice to continue or the choice to rest and recover.

The panic state

Like a game of "stress Buckaroo", the heavier the load on your body becomes, the more likely it is you're going to "blow"! Overloading with a number of external factors is not unusual, but when several loaded events occur over a relatively short period of time, the overload placed on your stress hormones can cause your body to go into a panic state!

Stress management is more than just increasing your stress threshold; it's also managing your ability to counteract the "usual" pattern of happenings that occur as a result of stress overload. Being able to break the negative pattern and "jump" out of a panic state into a more productive state means being able to *interrupt* the usual pattern.

Dealing with events that matter to you

When faced with stressful events, it's all too easy to get into a state where you're unable to see anything other than the negativity the event represents in your mind. When this happens, your mind becomes clouded and, to coin a phrase, you become "unable to see the wood for the trees". Clearly, it's important to be able to break out of this negative state of mind as quickly as possible in order to begin seeing positive ways in which you might resolve the situation.

Your ability to change your mind state is something that becomes easier with practice. Yes, life can be unfair at times and life can certainly bring about a number of situations you are not happy with, but when put into perspective in the grand scale of things, these are events that are likely to pale into insignificance.

Stressful triggers in life will happen, it's inevitable, and it isn't something you are able to change or control. However, something you *do* have *absolute* control over is the way in which you resolve and move on.

> Absolute – this is a trigger word I use, and a word that is part of my understanding process. When faced with a situation that can be interpreted as either good or bad, positive or negative, resourceful or not, I will always ask myself if I have *absolute* control over the outcome, based on my behaviour. In other words, I ask myself if my response can change the by-product of that situation to benefit me, and those around me, in the best way possible.

Stress credits

I myself have encountered stressful and depressing (I use this word with caution) situations in my life. Most of the time, these situations were the result of external events resisting the speed of my progress.

Just as a bank holds an account of your funds and the amount of money you have available to you at any one time, your body holds an account of the amount of stress it can tolerate at any given time. If you push those levels beyond acceptable, and effectively too far into the red, the interest will begin to accumulate until your account is closed down by the bank.

Taking care of your body by addressing the three key elements of stress management – lifestyle, nutrition and fitness – allows you to manipulate the deposits and withdrawals you make. The key to effective stress management is to ensure that more deposits are made than withdrawals.

 **Think**

Over the next week or so, think about the trigger situations that induce a stress state (withdrawal) and those that induce a euphoric state (deposit). Measure both and check the balance.

Once you have identified the deficit, you can take steps to increase the number of deposits and reduce the number of withdrawals. Remember: people experience stress in different ways and what induces a stress state for you may not do so for someone else.

Identify – Manage – Eliminate

Physical stress prompts

The human body is an amazing thing. When you start to consciously think about all the micro-adjustments it makes every millisecond, you begin to realize that hundreds of those tiny adjustments are being made even before the thought that prompted them is over. Considering this, your body is very efficient when it comes to letting you know or reminding you that something isn't working.

One of the most effective reminders used by the body is pain. For example, I recently bought a new pair of walking boots, but after just a few miles of walking in them the heels began to feel uncomfortable. I returned to my car to remove the boots and discovered that the skin on my heels had been rubbed painfully bare. Now, at the time of first feeling the pain I could have chosen to fight it and to continue my planned walk, but if I had done so the injury could potentially have become much worse and the recovery time needed greatly extended as a result. My decision to take note of the feeling of discomfort and to minimize the risk of further injury by returning to my car meant that I also minimized the amount of recovery time my body would need.

The above is a good example of physical stress assessment in action. It is essential that we take note of the messages sent out by our body; if something doesn't feel right, or there's an overload of stress, then pain will appear. The appearance of pain is a signal that you have a choice to make – the choice to continue or the choice to rest and recover.

Caveat: pain is a great motivator in a metaphorical and non-physical sense. For example, I made the choice while scrubbing dishes in a friend's restaurant to never let anyone tell me what I could or couldn't do in the future. I made the pain so unbearable (mentally) that my body channelled my thoughts into avoiding any situation that would result in experiencing that painful feeling. I call this "pain fixing" and it describes those "enough-is-enough" moments that most of us are familiar with.

As mentioned earlier, within our Western culture we generally only take action to fix something once we know it has broken. The well-known phrase, "If it's not broken, don't fix it", goes a long way towards explaining this deeply instilled way of thinking. However, while this way of thinking may have served us well during the industrial revolution, it's no longer appropriate in modern times and we cannot wait for things to break before we look into ways of improving them. In Eastern culture things are very different, and improvement or self-preservation is taken more seriously. When you think of Eastern cultures, it's easy to bring to mind the physical activities in which persons of all ages regularly take part to combat mental and physical impairments. Activities such as yoga, chi-gong (qigong), tai chi (t'ai chi ch'uan) and many others are all commonplace rituals and part of everyday life.

Stress isn't a weakness, it's a way of modern life.

It's a popular misconception that suffering from stress is a form of weakness, but this is a false belief that must be avoided. Stress is a natural event that everyone will encounter at least once in their working day, but not all of us will *suffer* from its effects. The only difference between those who suffer and those who don't is *choice*; we all have the choice of whether or not to suffer.

Why is stress on the increase?

Well, it only takes a look at modern day living to work out why stress is on the increase. Obesity is on the increase; the national debt is rising; terminal illnesses and cancer-related deaths are on the increase; our overall health as a nation is deteriorating; so, all things considered, stress seems inevitable! With this in mind, we need to look again at what stress actually is.

So what is stress, exactly?

As discussed already, there are many different forms of stress, so your personal definition depends largely on your overall experience of life thus far. These individual factors not only create differences in terms of tolerance to stress but also in the outcomes of stress in each case. For example, an inner city business person may experience stress in a completely different form to a rural business person. Each will experience stress in their working day but the sources of the stress will be different. One person's stressors are not necessarily the same as the next person's, and what one person copes with on a daily basis may push another over the edge! However, the meaning is the same in each case; each individual experiences their own definition of stress.

It's worth noting at this point that the word "stress" has not always been used in the way it is today in modern language. It is in fact a word that was widely used within physics, describing the amount of tension force that can be applied before a weakness is shown. This "weakness" – or "indifference" as I prefer to call it – is where the transition in language took place and how the modern meaning came to be adopted. However, as you know already, stress is *not* a weakness.

To stress or not to stress, that is the question!

It's fair to say that some people are naturally more "stressy" than others and because of this there may be people you knowingly choose to avoid in potentially stressful situations such as family events or parties. Over the years, a lot of research has gone into categorizing people with these sorts of traits into certain "personality types" but I see this as simply overcomplicating things. Labelling individuals in this way should be avoided as a label can be very hard to shake off and people often become accustomed to working within its boundaries as a consequence.

For me, we are all one. Yes, we act differently during certain situations but this is simply down to how we have been programmed to cope during those situations. For example, both of my children enjoy riding their bikes. One is four years older than the other but the youngest becomes frustrated when she cannot cycle as fast as her brother. However, it's not frustration that's the issue, but subsequent behaviour. My task as a parent is to re-educate her so that she understands the restrictions she faces are not through fault but through simple human restraints – in this case, age and strength.

Avoid labelling a person as stressed, or anything else for that matter, for they will usually live up to it.

Are some people more open to stress than others?

In simple terms, the answer to the above question is "yes" – yes, some people are more open to stress or perhaps more open to "inviting" stress, but only on the basis of past learning. We all *learn* how to act in certain situations or how to respond to certain happenings, and what we learn becomes imprinted in our neurology. However, what can be learned can also be *un*-learned, so we can learn to respond with stress or without stress.

According to research carried out at the University of Maryland Medical Center in the US, the factors that most influence an individual's response to stress include the following:

- **Genetics** – evidence suggests that some individuals are genetically predisposed to stress, with some having a more efficient relaxation response than others.
- **Personality** – different personality traits cause different people to respond differently to stressful events. Evidence suggests that having a more outgoing personality

can help to lower levels of stress-related inflammatory hormones in an individual and thereby improve their response to stress.

- **Early years nurturing** – individuals experiencing childhood abuse may have long-term hypothalamic-pituitary system abnormalities, which affects their ability to regulate stress.
- **Disease** – certain immune regulated diseases (eczema and rheumatoid arthritis for example) can cause an individual to be more susceptible to stress.
- **Prolonged exposure** – the more intense the stressor and the longer the exposure to it, the more harmful the effects in an individual.

The groups of individuals who are more vulnerable to the effects of stress compared to others include the following:

- **Older adults** – age affects the efficiency of the relaxation response, making it more difficult to return to a "calm" state after a stressful event. Older adults are often exposed to stressors such as the death of a loved one or major health issues.
- **Women** – all women, but working mothers in particular, have been found to face higher levels of stress. This is thought to be down to a typically heavier workload in everyday life.
- **Widows or divorced individuals** – a number of independent studies have shown that married people have a greater life expectancy than widowed or divorced people.
- **Individuals with lower levels of education.**

- **Unemployed individuals** – the long-term unemployed in particular and anyone experiencing financial difficulties.
- **Lonely or isolated individuals.**
- **Individuals facing discrimination.**
- **City dwellers in general.**

 **Task**

Within the next few moments, attempt to become stressful about a situation. Focus your mind on how it feels to be stressed and experience the associated thoughts and emotions.

Now break the above state by focusing your mind on experiencing a positive outcome to the stressful situation.

What did you notice?

....
....
....
....

How quickly were you able to change the state?

....
....
....
....

(Continued)

What differences did you notice?

....

....

....

....

What benefits will the ability to break your stressful state bring
  you in the future?

....

....

....

....

Letting go of the now

It can be very easy at times to hold on to the past, particularly past events or happenings that have affected our lives to
this point either negatively or positively. In order to move forwards and to become better established to stress less, you need
to understand and accept that you have little control over the
past or the future. In fact, when you think about it, there is
very little that you *can* control. Think about this:

> You can't control the past as that moment has gone. As you
> are reading this text you are in the present, but the present has
> already passed as each word you read no longer represents
> the present, therefore it becomes the past. The future is the
> next word ahead and as you read it, it becomes the present
> and the past at almost the same time. You now no longer have
> control over the beginning of this paragraph; you do not have

the ability to change the choice to read it, but you do have the choice over whether you continue reading in the present to get to the future. You have the choice to stop, not read the next few words, and therefore not make the future happen. That choice is now in the past as you have continued to read; many choices have passed, none of which you now have control over. You cannot delete reading the first line of this paragraph, nor the middle; the only choice you had is now in the past. You can either regret not making that choice or you can simply let it go ... it's the past ... the past has no direct value over the present, apart from the choice to either continue on this path or stop ... .

How we see ourselves

I am often asked whether or not the way we look has any bearing on the amount of stress we can deal with. My response is very simple, and remains the same irrespective of an individual's past, or their learnt behaviours.

Stress, and your ability to manage it, is directly linked to your appearance.

How?

Well, we all have an internal representation of who we are and it's this perception – or how we see ourselves – that triggers our internal beliefs in terms of what we *think* we can deal with. This is something that affects more than just your ability to deal with stress because it also controls everyone around you.

For example, early in my career I was working with a lady who had some internal issues about her relationship and the ability she had to connect with her husband. As we worked through the session, it became apparent that she was hitting a barrier when it came to communicating with him effectively, which was thus making her "stressed". After running through some progressive activities, I asked if he would consider coming in, suggesting she could invite him to a future session. She immediately dismissed it, saying, "He isn't the type of man who would go to therapy." "What type of man is he then?" I asked ... the session continued.

Several weeks later I received a call from the husband and he asked if he could come and talk with me. During our appointment we worked on some very key issues that, in a nutshell, revolved around his learned interpretation of what and how a "real man" should act, and how this had created a persona that was being reflected in his behaviour. After running though a number of future scenarios, he began to appreciate how his interpretation of his behaviour/actions created a barrier, and how it resulted in his inability to deal with or understand stress. After this light-bulb moment he made the choice to open up to his wife and to explain the reasons why.

This was a major milestone for both of them. His past learning had resulted in his resistance to change, but both of them were now able to release the stress and to improve their relationship as a result.

Your thoughts become your behaviours.

My reason for mentioning this is that while you may be the one *doing* stress, the trigger may be an external factor that you have *limited* control over – not *absolute* control – so your stress may be attributed to, or worsened by, an external factor. This means, to a certain degree, that the choice you have is whether to continue putting yourself in that situation or whether to take the action to address it. In the previous example, the choice was to make a joint effort to identify the issue and then take action to address it – avoiding it was no longer an option.

Knowing when to stress

As with many things, it is good to know the situations that bring about the problems.

 **Think**

Over the next few days, make a mental note of the situations in which you are most stressed. You might also find it beneficial to write out a physical list of the most stressful situations. Look for the key triggers (stressors), keeping in mind that there may be more than one stacked. Each time you identify an issue, ask yourself, "What can I do right now to ensure this doesn't affect me in this way again?"

(*Continued*)

Keeping this type of record allows you to draw a map. The map can be thought of as an activity schedule that clearly highlights the time of day and the lead experience before the trigger. Mapping this activity means you create the choice to either divert or to repeat that journey with the knowledge of what lies ahead.

Tip: You may find it helpful to list the stressors on a sliding scale relating to the impact of the stress. For example, on a scale of 1–10, a score of 10 represents almost unbearable stress (at collapsing point) and a score of 1 represents a mildly annoying but ultimately manageable level of stress.

Remember – you *do* stress; it takes a large amount of effort to create all of those negative, unproductive emotions.

Stressors ... what really matters?

As we have discovered, stress is something that is individual to each of us and experienced in different ways depending on how we choose to react to it. However, there are several common stressors that are generically labelled as stressful times. Something that is important to remember here is that labels, once given, are hard to shake off.

Common "labelled" stressors include:

- Housing – moving house, relocating, buying and selling property, etc.
- Financial difficulties

- Relationships – including relationship breakdown and divorce
- Major life events – marriage, starting a family, etc.
- Career – unemployment, promotion, change, education, etc.
- Loss – loss of a family member, loved one, beloved animal, etc.
- Illness/injury – personal or close family member
- Theft – or becoming a victim of any crime
- Festive/holiday periods
- Children leaving home – empty nest syndrome

When looking at these, you may notice one or two that particularly resonate with you and some that may be affecting your life currently. No matter what the source, the process of elimination, or what I prefer to call the process of *understanding*, always remains the same.

"The stronger man takes the choice to walk away from a fight, knowing the choice had been taken away from his opponent."

More interesting stats on stress ...

A team of Harvard University researchers compiled a "Top 10" list of the most common stressors in everyday life. They are as follows:

1. Always running late/never having enough time
2. Feelings of frustration and/or anger

3. Feelings of doubt over your ability to do something
4. Feeling overextended
5. Lack of time for relaxation/stress relief
6. Feeling tense
7. Negative thinking/pessimistic outlook
8. Family conflicts
9. Experiencing physical and/or emotional burnout
10. Feeling lonely

The difference between major and minor stressors ... is there a difference?

In a word, "no"! In my world, a stressor is a stressor: there is no difference. Sure, there are events/stressors that score differently on your stress chart than others but ultimately they all have the same emotional outcome. Look at it this way – being late for an appointment could cause an element of stress, but so could being early!

Choice

When I worked in the estate agency world, the word "stress" was often bandied around as if it was something to be *expected* and something that should be considered the norm. I would hear people say things such as, "moving is the most stressful time" or "I am so stressed" or "I am never moving again" on a daily basis. I used to feel sorry for the property owners who would be all set to move, only to lose their buyer just a few weeks before the planned moving date. It wasn't nice for them, and it certainly wasn't nice having to break the news to them. However, one thing I learned early on in this environment was that it didn't matter how much anger, frustration or emotional resentment was thrown about, you couldn't convince someone to buy something they didn't want to. Yes, it was annoying; yes, a lot of time, money and emotion had usually gone in to the process by this point, but no amount of negativity could resolve it. In fact, nothing could effectively resolve a situation in which the chain had already broken.

The lesson I learned through this experience was that things follow a simple path. Is it really worth losing sleep over something or becoming physically and mentally ill over something that will happen anyway? Wouldn't it be better to focus the negative energy into something more positive and of much better use? For example, in the previous scenario, this would be finding a new buyer. When working in that environment, I would sometimes be told that I was blasé about the situation, and I would be asked how I could just get on as if nothing had happened. My response remains the same to this day: there is no point in crying over spilt milk.

Consciously, we can have as much control over how we perform and adapt to situations as we want. As I have said, we have the choice … to stress or not to stress. You can look at an event and draw only negativity from it or you can look at it and draw strength and learning from it. You always have the choice.

 **Task**

Your task, as you progress through the following weeks, is to use the phrase below whenever you feel you've reached a score of 3 or higher on your stress scale:

"*I am* .... *about that but now I am not.*"

(For example: I am angry/frustrated/upset/hurt/stressed about that but now I am not.)

By repeating this affirmation, you can change the emotions instantly. It may take a few attempts, but persevere. The more you practise, the easier it becomes and the faster you will be able to alter the outcome/behaviour.

Don't mask stress

We are now a society that tends to mask/cover stress rather than face/deal with it. When clients come to see me, many of them will have seen another therapist or someone different in the past. The first thing they notice on arrival is that my approach is quite different and, as it's a no-nonsense approach, it can come as a bit of a shock!

If you are new to my work, let me just say that I am someone who is more likely to ask you to get up and move on if you happen to be slumped on the floor, rather than someone who might take the more conventional approach of asking you if you're okay first, or employing the softly-softly tact of telling you that everything is going to be okay.

You see, for me, there is nothing more frustrating than masking an issue – or attempting to avoid dealing with the root cause – rather than dealing with it head on. The good news is that by being someone who has chosen to read this book, you are someone who has already come to realize that things don't have to be as they are; they can be *better*. In reading this book, you've realized that you're unhappy with the label of stress sufferer, and you know that there can be a life without it. You are someone who is looking for answers, and for this I congratulate you.

Coping, masking, or covering – none of this offers the answer to a stress-free life; instead, it represents a move towards accepting that you want to *keep* stress in your life.

Attention seeking ...

This is a controversial topic, but one that needs to be addressed nonetheless. There are some who use stress and other associated/labelled illnesses to gain attention. This fault is something that merits an entire book to itself but for now I feel it is something that's relevant to the content of this book and therefore requires a brief overview.

Avoid, at all costs, using stress as a tool to gain attention. Falling into this trap allows the mind to create a victim mentality, and this is something that has no benefit or support. Of course, there may be a certain element of enjoyment gained from the attention, but the value of it (either positive or negative) is negative.

Think about it this way:

Andy Murray wins Wimbledon after years of hard work, knockbacks and dedication. The attention he receives post-achievement is positive. He has worked hard to obtain the title and his commitment to achieving it has meant making certain sacrifices along the way.

Billy (a fictional character) adopts a victim approach; he works hard to maintain this representation and achieves a certain level of attention as a result. He makes certain sacrifices to stay in this character and will at every opportunity accept fate as a reason to build upon and confirm his belief that others are much more fortunate.

Now, when you look at the very basics of the above, both work hard, both make sacrifices, and both have similarities in their strategy. The only major difference is that one makes the conscious choice to look at the positive value, and the other looks only at the negative value. Both of them are building on something, yet they are achieving very different levels of attention.

 **Think**

When working within your stress management programme, be aware of adopting any state other than a positive one. If you feel you are jumping into a negative value state, then it's time to question your actions. For example:

Why am I actually doing this?
What positive values will this bring?

Changing the way you ask a question can then change the results it will bring. The more positive the questions and the more questions you ask, the more positive the outcomes will become. Also, change the statements you make about yourself. For example:

Change, "Today I am feeling stressed," to "What am I going to do today to ensure I live my day without stress?"

These simple but very effective linguistic changes will radically change the direction of your thoughts and in turn your reality.

Note: Re-educating your mind to think in this positive form will be a conscious choice at first, but after a while it will be followed at a subconscious level.

Task

Think of two situations that would normally cause you to adopt a stressful state:

1. ....
....
....

2. ....
....
....

(For example: I am angry/frustrated/upset/hurt/stressed about that but now I am not.)

Now list what happens within your body:

1. ....
....
....
....
....
....

(Example: my chest becomes tight and my breathing rate increases.)

Now list what happens within your mind:

1. ....
....
....

2. ....
....
....

(Example: I can see the words on the page, my mind feels focused towards this and my mind becomes flustered.) Now FLIP that situation to produce a positive outcome:

1. ....
....
....

2. ....
....
....

(Example: I know that the letter is chasing me for money, but I am doing my best and have spoken to them and explained my situation. They will have to wait and I will let them know when my situation improves; any spare money I have will be spent on clearing the debt so I can finally put this behind me. That letter when opened is going in my file.)

The seed has the future already stored within it, it simply requires nurture.

I strongly advocate incorporating all three essential elements into your future, just as I have done in my life and as many others experiencing an equally challenging journey have done.

There was a time in my life where I had no money, was working three jobs, had a child on the way, and was underweight.

I made a choice, while washing dishes one night, to never let anyone tell me what I could or couldn't do; I wouldn't let stress, anger or resentment keep me down and I would fight for what I believe was my God-given right – to be happy.

And more thought-provoking stats on stress ...

In the UK, work-related stress is defined as follows: "A harmful reaction people have to undue pressures and demands placed on them at work." The following statistics are from the results of the UK Labour Force Survey in 2011/2012.

- Stress accounted for 40 per cent of all work-related illnesses.
- The industries most affected by stress-related illness were education, social work, public administration and defence.
- The occupations with the highest reported work-related stress illnesses were the healthcare profession, nurses in particular; teaching and education; the caring profession and housing association and welfare workers in particular.
- The main sources of work-related stress were reported to be pressure, lack of support from managers/superiors and workplace bullying.

In the US, the results of the fifth annual Labor Day survey revealed the following:

- More than 50 per cent of the American workforce experience feelings of being "somewhat" or "extremely" stressed at work.
- And one in six workers reported feeling frustrated or angry enough at work to want to "hit a co-worker".

So what is burnout ... ?

Prolonged periods of physical stress along with psychological stress can lead to what's known as burnout, and psychological stress can be defined as follows ...

"Psychological stress occurs when perceived demands, threats or fears outweigh the perceived capabilities or benefits."

The key to counteracting burnout is to accept that you can't always control everything in your outer environment but you can choose to control your inner environment by choosing to see "challenges" in place of "threats" whenever possible. A simple linguistic change can focus your mind on looking for solutions rather than getting bogged down with your thoughts focused on perceived threats.

At Dartmouth College in the US, researchers carried out two experiments to assess the effects of "standing out" in the workplace. The focus of the studies was to monitor the effects of being put in a position of "going against the grain" in the workplace and being noticed more as a result. For some people, standing out and being noticed was a source of stress, but for others it provided a more positive source of motivation. The researchers concluded that in order to feel motivated rather than stressed, an individual must feel *challenged* by a situation rather than *threatened*.

In a nutshell, the way you look at a situation – challenge or threat – is linked directly to the outcome of the situation. Changing the way you look at things can make the difference between a perceived threat remaining a source of stress, or a perceived challenge being overcome.

Changing threat to challenge can change stress to eustress.

Eustress = the type of stress that revs you up and makes you feel positive about yourself and life. It can make you look forward to a potential challenge rather than fear it. Many individuals feel that eustress is an essential element of getting the creative juices flowing and giving a task their best effort.

Step Three

PREVENTION AND OPTIMIZATION

"I've had a lot of worries in my life, most of which never happened."

– *Mark Twain*

Stress is nothing more than a behavioural state ...

Change the way you stand!

The mind – body connection goes beyond mind to body because it also works in the opposite direction. The body to mind connection is equally important: in fact, it has been proven in studies that emotions can be changed, simply by making small adjustments to your form.

 **Task**

Take note of the way you are sitting or standing right now:

Are you slumping in your seat with rounded shoulders, or are you standing tall?

(*Continued*)

Are you restricting the amount of oxygen your body is able to take in with your poor posture, or are you allowing good posture to help your body breathe freely?

For the next few moments, pay attention to each separate part of your body. Start at your feet and work your way up towards your head, taking your attention from one part of your body to the next and noting how each area feels. Note how the muscles feel in each area, and make a conscious effort to release any tension or tightness you become aware of.

Tip: Most people find it beneficial to close their eyes while doing this exercise, and listening to relaxing music can help to create a calm and controlled breathing rate.

Staying in a stress-free state

Disassociate yourself from any environment that does not positively complement your stress-free state. With this in mind, it's also important to avoid spending time with people who appear to "suffer" stress in a similar way to you. It's very common for individuals to find shelter among others displaying similar emotions to themselves as it can bring about a sense of belonging. However, this type of belonging is something you should remove yourself from, as it is essentially a negative form of social acceptance. It's this sort of acceptance that's largely to blame for the current obesity health crisis and all of the associated stresses created by the "blame culture" in modern society. Remember, you become like those you mix with the most ... the more you mix with stress-free, happy, motivated and enthusiastic people the more you will adopt those positive traits.

As a point of interest, a study carried out in 2011 at the University of Hawaii concluded that stress is as contagious as the common cold!

Once you have changed the people you mix with, it's then time to take the "new you" to the next level; it's time to become the alpha person. What I mean by this is that it's time to be the dominant person, able to control not only yourself in difficult situations but also others. However, this does not mean becoming a bully or the bossy person who attempts to call all the shots, it means becoming the more reserved go-to person who brings value to a situation with everything they say.

For every finger you point there are always three pointing directly back at you.

Becoming the alpha person

Doing this is simpler than you think. Take a moment to think about animals and the body language and postures they use to demonstrate how they fit into the "pecking order" around others.

 **Think**

Now picture someone who has just won a race. The race winner will generally lift their hands high and stand tall; their body visibly changes in that moment of success and their outward posture allows others to see their internal feelings of achievement. Of course, I am not suggesting that you walk around with your hands held high at all times; I'm suggesting you think about winners ... think about the presence they have and the ability they have to take charge and to control a room as a result.

Now flip your thoughts and think about someone who has just lost a race, or perhaps picture yourself at a time when you were feeling low ... how does the body posture change? How do people act when they feel deflated? How about when they feel stressed?

People generally tighten themselves up under such circumstances, attempting to become as small as they can. They roll their shoulders in; they reduce the amount of oxygen their body can bring in, creating a change in their voice as a result, and they look down in an effort to avoid making eye contact.

Avoid being the shy dog, start being the wolf ...

Make yourself big. Open up and make yourself as big as you can. Make a role change from a place of non-power to power and a posture of powerless to powerful. Look others in the eye and make the connection. Use your voice to show that you mean business ... express yourself and take feedback on the response.

But does it work when you fake it?

Yes, it does. When you change your non-verbal cues to create a positive outlook, it registers within your neurological pathways and this generates the release of "feel-good" hormones. Athletes have used this form of visualization for years, and there are many commonly used phrases such as "seeing is believing" that serve to remind us of the power of the mind. In this sense, "faking it till you make it" is simply pushing the proven concept of visualization a little further.

... and how do I become the wolf?

Think about the places where stress would usually take control: imagine for a moment your non-verbal communication or how you would communicate with yourself on the inside ... and now think about how that is transmitted on the outside.

Now change that negative internal communication and self-talk into a positive format. For example, let's say you're feeling stressed about an upcoming event and you're chewing your fingernails to the bone thinking about all the things that might go wrong whilst saying to yourself, "What if it all goes wrong?" Or, "I'm going to look like an idiot." Your mind is full of pictures of what things are going to look like when they go wrong. Stop! You can change all of this into a positive format by changing the pictures in your mind into images of how things are going to look when they go right, and how you're going to look when everything is a success, whilst saying to yourself, "What if it all goes right?" Imagine yourself at the event with everything going perfectly and visualize how you will look when you experience the achievement. When you do this, notice every small change in your body and your posture, and notice the differences between you feeling like an idiot and you feeling like the perfect you.

Knowing who you *can* be as the "perfect you" is something I describe as "core identity". Core identity is the most important aspect of projection. Confidence grows from this point and it influences the flow of communication both internally and externally.

Non-verbal communication – the way you act is the way you perform.

Take a moment to think about the last time you were talking to someone about a passion of yours: were you talking freely, confidently and with dominance? The likelihood is that you were, so why is that? Well, you were talking about something you knew about in detail. The information and the subsequent reactions experienced when talking about a common topic are produced from your core identity – a place where your feelings and emotions flow in a positive state.

Instead of *doing* stress, *do* your new body until you become what you need.

No regrets ... ?

Never regret the time you spend doing the things you want.

"The mark of a successful man is one that has spent an entire day on the bank of a river without feeling guilty about it."

Author Unknown

In years to come, looking back and wondering why you lived with stress and wasted so much time over it is more than likely going to be a source of frustration for you, but you're not alone with that. Here are just a few of the most commonly made "wish list" statements:

I wish I hadn't worked so hard, and spent more time with my family.
I wish I'd stayed in contact with my friends and family.
I wish I could have allowed myself to be happy.
I wish I had the courage to be the person I really wanted.
I wish I had done what I wanted rather than what society said I should.

Thinking, but not …

Rest your mind on a regular basis, and listen to your subconscious mind within these times. I have spent many hours in the last few years digesting masses of information and then just listening to my thoughts. This is something I might do by taking my dog for a walk or going for a run along the beach, and it's often during these times of solitude that my mind works out a lot of the information and restructures my thinking. Stress, as we have established, is something we all have the ability to do, but educating yourself in terms of knowing and understanding which symptoms to look out for allows you to block the trigger thought and break the negative cycle in the process.

A simple walk may seem so trivial but exercise in any form and taking care of your fitness in general is more than just keeping yourself looking good and feeling confident, it's also providing a golden opportunity for your mind to rest and to process the information you are constantly learning.

Stronger, braver, happier

There are many stories of people around the world who have faced horrific situations and then bounced back stronger, perhaps braver and certainly a lot happier. These stories of post-traumatic growth highlight that your stress management is your choice to make yourself better; it is your very springboard to success … so use it. Once you have encountered something as serious as stress, you can then use the experience to make yourself much stronger.

Think

Think about the "wish list" statements listed earlier and consider how you could flip them into a positive format.

For example:

The negative statement, "I wish I hadn't worked so hard, and spent more time with my family" could be flipped into, "I will spend more time with my family." Or, "I wish I had stayed in contact with my friends and family," could be flipped into, "I will re-establish contact with at least one friend."

Consider your thoughts on your own "wish list" statements; can you flip them into positives?

Task

Starting today, practise the following exercises. As you do this, notice the differences and the outcomes each exercise brings and assess how these have changed your day. Certain aspects of the exercises may suit some more than others, and that's

(Continued)

fine, but attempt to experience all of them at least once, and then continue to practise those that bring about a better feeling for the following 21 days. If you need to – and it may help – create cards and keep them in your wallet or purse, or perhaps on a sticky note attached to your computer screen. Either way, keep the cards or notes somewhere conspicuous so that they will serve to remind you at least twice an hour to carry out the task. The key to success is re-educating the mind to deliver the messages you want.

Exercises:

1. **Become a winner** – change your non-verbal communication by standing or sitting tall. Be consciously aware of your stance today and notice how powerful these slight changes can be. Open up your chest and make yourself the dominant one, even if you are alone.

2. **Challenge your mind at least twice a day** – this can be by playing games that promote competition or using mind game apps or books. Some of my clients have chosen to learn six new words per day in a foreign language; three in the morning and three in the evening. Whatever choices you make, ensure you commit to this time; for those using public transport to commute to and from work, journey time is often prime in terms of dedicated mind challenge time.

3. **Watch or learn something that triggers positive emotions** – this can be looking back at any media footage that produces "positive" emotions; it must be powerful enough to ensure you reach the point of experiencing a genuine smile. Perhaps pictures of

your children or your family, or even YouTube clips of amazing events. Whatever you choose, do this at least once during your day.

4. **Gratitude** – it is amazing how a simple "thank you" can change the dynamics of those around you or the perception others have of you. The act of thanking others or of showing gratitude is one that's demonstrated less and less frequently within modern society; however, simply opening or holding a door for a stranger can have a ripple effect. Sure, it doesn't rub off on everyone, but the more you practise doing it yourself the more you will experience it in return (this is a principle known as the Law of Attraction). Watch how quickly your emotions change as you thank others.

5. **Enjoy stress freedom** – your ultimate goal is to wipe out negativity by replacing *any* negative emotions you experience with three positive emotions. This means that for every one thought you have that makes you feel bad, you need to think of three things that make you feel good. If you do this for *every* negative thought on a daily basis, you will quickly remove all associated negativity from your "memory bank".

When you take the time to practice and follow through with these exercises, you no longer dwell on thoughts that lead to feelings of stress or anxiety but consciously think about the dreams and visions you have created for yourself instead, thereby keeping your thoughts on the positive aspects of your life.

A note on the Law of Attraction:

In a nutshell, the Law of Attraction can be summed up by the old adage, "What goes around comes around," or, in other words, every positive effort attracts a positive return.

Change your thinking ... it isn't that way, it's this way!

Positive psychology is the term used to describe a branch of psychology that focuses on promoting mental health rather than solely treating mental illness. In a nutshell, the goal of positive psychology is to positively change the way an individual *feels* through changing how they *think*. The founder of positive psychology, Martin Seligman, defines his work as, *"The scientific study of positive human functioning and flourishing on multiple levels that include the biological, personal, relational, institutional, cultural and global dimensions of life,"* or, in other words, positive psychology is all about achieving a life of happiness and fulfilment. In his words, the purpose of promoting good mental health is *"to make normal life more fulfilling"* and it's his use of the word "normal" that's of key importance.

Stress is linked to normal. Normal is average.

Stress is the average; statistics are based on the average.

Don't be the average!

If you slip into feeling content with your "average" status, you stop striving for *better* than average, therefore you forfeit the opportunity to experience better than average levels of happiness or the true contentment of living a truly fulfilling life.

"If you do not raise your eyes, you will think that you are the highest point."

Antonio Porchia

Consider the following:

- 10 per cent of your happiness is the result of your outside world.
- 90 per cent of your happiness is the result of your internal world.

When you take the above statistics on board, you realize that working harder to achieve external success is not the way to achieve internal success.

Some fascinating stats on happiness ...

According to the World Database of Happiness, you are likely to be happier if ...

- You are in a relationship, a long-term relationship in particular.
- You have a close circle of friends – the number of friends is unimportant.
- You take an active interest in, or you're engaged in, politics.

- You drink in moderation – moderate drinkers are statistically happier than non-drinkers.
- You consider yourself to be good-looking, irrespective of whether you *actually* are, objectively speaking.
- And you don't commute to work.

The results of a German study revealed a link between the amount of time a person spends commuting to and from work and their level of satisfaction with life. It was found that individuals who had a commute of one hour or more into work each day were much less happy than non-commuting individuals. The results also suggest that earning more money in a job that's further from home does not compensate for the hours lost in transit.

However, the database researchers are keen to point out that none of us should expect to feel happy all of the time, making it clear that sadness acts an indicator to change the pattern of thinking or behaviour that's causing it. According to their findings, feeling sad around 10 per cent of the time is actually good for us!

Interestingly, the research findings also show that exercising after work makes us much happier than sinking into the sofa with a beer.

Drawing a blank

There are times when all you need to do to create clarity in your mind is simply pick up a piece of blank paper and a pen.

This is something I often do when working with clients and I have found that there are many things that can be resolved by simply getting thoughts down on paper.

Stress mapping ...

The idea behind mapping out your stress pathway is to allow your mind to experience a sense of release – release from any restraints and release from holding negativity in. The advantage of using this technique over many others is that it can be done anytime and anywhere.

 **Task**

Before you start, there are a few things you need to consider: avoid starting this exercise if you are in a stressful state or any other state apart from one that is going to be productive. If this is going to be difficult, spend at least 10 minutes in meditation or quiet thinking, before starting. Do this in a quiet place where you can be alone without any distractions, and choose somewhere that will bring about a sense of peace such as a park, beach or anywhere else where your mind can filter out the noise of modern life.

When you are ready, take a few minutes to bring your attention to your breathing. Relax all of the muscles in your body

(Continued)

and clear your mind ... take just 10 deep breaths, relaxing a little more each time ... now you are ready ...

Start in any way you wish, for example; I "do" stress when

....

List all of the reasons for your feelings of stress, or perhaps create a spider diagram in place of writing a list, and map them out in a way that will allow you to categorize them at the end. When working with clients, I would usually plan these out on separate pieces of paper with the following titles, but you can work in any way that best suits your strategy.

1. Personal Growth
2. Fun and Recreation
3. Physical Environment
4. Business/Career
5. Health and Fitness
6. Family and Friends
7. Romance

You may find that it takes several attempts to complete all of the above; in some cases clients have found it better to complete one section per day. The key is to be flexible in your approach, to release any pressure and demonstrate complete honesty.

As with any aspect of change, it is essential to keep honesty at the forefront of your consciousness at all times. I meet many clients who "beat around the bush" when it comes to finally letting go of emotions and truths. Be honest from day one. If stress is hidden within a certain part of you that is emotionally negative, then it's definitely time to rid yourself of it forever. The more you work through this the easier it will become, but start as you mean to go on.

When looking at the previous seven topics, you may note that one of the most largely blamed stressors has been left out ...

8. Finance

Finance should always be discussed separately or outside of the seven topics as it can often become an overwhelming "blamer" for other issues if introduced during the other topical areas. Although our financial situation is often given as the primary reason for becoming stressful in many of the other areas, when digging deeper you will actually realize that although it does have a large impact, it very rarely contributes as much as you think, making it the easy option in terms of attributing blame.

For example, a common stressor in terms of lacking motivation to take part in an activity is a lack of funds. An individual might believe that in order to "feel" motivated they *must* have sufficient funds to take part in the first place or they *need* to receive some kind of financial reward at the end of it all. The reality is that motivation is simply a state of clarity when attempting a particular task, and nothing to do with financial gain. Sure, if you were motivated to cross a bridge, when fearful of heights, by a financial reward waiting for you on the other side then you could say receiving the reward added purpose to the task but, in truth, you would have crossed the bridge without the financial reward if you had the clarity of being chased by a hungry tiger, for example!

Avoid pointing the money finger, as money has no ability to make you "feel" anything; it's the emotions you have added to the ownership of "money" that produces the behaviour.

Becoming stressed at children/partners is another very common example. The lack of understanding or communication seems to be a very realistic trigger/stressor, and not being heard is certainly very frustrating. However, having worked with many people within this field, I often find it's not the third party to blame, but more the "stressed" individual's interpretation of the communication. If previous attempts to discuss a topic have failed or resulted in arguments, then any future attempt to discuss this topic will bring about the preconceived idea that any similar conversations will bring about the same results. In truth, this may not be the case; however, your subconscious will remind you of the past, and thus your behaviour when entering into that situation will usually pick up where it last left off.

When this is the case, the solution is not to "win" but to break" the pattern and resolve the situation. Simple ownership over changing the lead-in or approach to the conversation is perhaps all that's required to change the outcome. For example, "I want to change the way we ended up last time and see if we might just resolve it." Identifying the key triggers in all situations is absolutely vital and, again, it simply comes down to "choice" and "ownership" over each given event.

Legacy setting

In my book, *How To Change Your Life*, I discuss the process of ensuring that we work towards a legacy rather than a goal (or goals). The same principle applies to the effective management of stress and the ability to move forward with motivation and purpose.

Why legacy over goals ... ?

Well, a legacy lasts forever whereas goals are set with boundaries and generally end when the goal has been achieved. A legacy goes on beyond your lifetime, but you're probably wondering why this is important and how it relates to stress. Think about it this way: how do you want to be known and remembered? Take a look at the following words and think about how others would describe you now *and* how you would like to be remembered in, say, 60 years! By simply focusing your mind on these key words, you realign your subconscious mind to fulfil that legacy.

Task

Write just five key words that describe how others see you now:

1. ....
2. ....

(Continued)

3. ....

4. ....

5. ....

Now choose just 10 key words from the list below to describe how you would like to be known in the future:

Absorbing, Abundance, Admirable, Alive, Amazing, Appealing, Beautiful, Brilliant, Charming, Clear, Colourful, Confidence, Delightful, Deluxe, Dependable, Desire, Diamond, Discerning, Distinctive, Dynamic, Efficient, Enticing, Excellent, Exceptional, Exciting, Fair, Famous, Fantastic, Fascinating, Fashionable, Fetching, Free, Friendly, Full, Fun, Generous, Genius, Gentle, Glamorous, Glorious, Gorgeous, Graceful, Grand, Great, Happy, Healthy, Impressive, Incredible, Inspire, Interesting, Invigorating, Invincible, Inviting, Irresistible, Kind, Legend, Lucky, Memorable, Mighty, Natural, Outrageous, Outstanding, Passionate, Perfect, Popular, Positive, Precious, Proud, Pure, Radiant, Ravishing, Real, Refined, Reliable, Renowned, Seductive, Sensitive, Shy, Special, Spectacular, Strong, Stunning, Stylish, Superb, Terrific, Traditional, True, Trustworthy, Unbeatable, Unblemished, Unique, Valuable, Vigorous, Warm, Whole, Wise, Wonderful, Worthy, Youthful.

1. ....

2. ....

3. ....

4. ....

5. ....

6. ....

7. ....

8. ....
9. ....
10. ....

It's worth noting at this point that external factors will change in the future and the words may change as well, especially when you start to accomplish and achieve the foundations of each of the emotional attachments to those words.

Create a better picture

It's common practice to assume that you make decisions based on your internal representation of an event, thus creating an internal picture. This being said, you can easily relate stressful thinking to stressful visions of the current event or circumstance. As mentioned previously, the words you use in your description are in fact those that you have chosen to describe the internal image you have created.

 **Task**

Take a moment to think about the following image and write the caption that first springs to mind.

(*Continued*)

Now look at the picture again and flip your description to think in the opposite.

Now look at the picture again and describe it in the most positive perspective.

> Look at the three different captions and identify your thinking for each of them: what first sprung to mind? Did you see a bank robber, or a man in fancy dress, or perhaps a refuse collector? Did you see an adult or a child, a man or a woman?

The truth is that it's simply a cartoon of a person carrying what appear to be sacks. However, the mind, within a microsecond of viewing that image, fired off a number of past "knowns" and created a fake perception of what it thought the truth was.

How is this related to stress? Well, think back to the stressors and the situations that you listed as being stressful. How can you, moving forward, view these differently? What questions can you ask yourself that will change the negative value to a positive one? How can you ensure that you STOP thinking negatively and begin to see life only from a positive perspective?

Reality check: Obviously there will be times in life when it is simply impossible to see the situation through rose-tinted glasses; however, when times reach this level, follow the three Ps.

The three "P"s

1. **Pause** – pause for a moment and take another view of the situation. Would it, under different circumstances or on another day, create the "stress" emotions that it

is creating at the moment? If it wouldn't, then take the conscious choice to change it! If it would, then "flip" it and ask yourself: what positives can I learn from this experience?

2. **Perspective** – put it into perspective. Think back to the "stress scale" you created earlier, with a score of 10 representing the worst that could happen and a score of 1 representing something that's marginally annoying but ultimately manageable. Remember, these are only emotions that you are controlling; the emotions you have attached to the event. When you start to look at a situation and you grade it according to your stress scale chart, the likelihood is that something you thought was "unbearably" stressful doesn't actually merit a score of more than 2 in the grand scale of things!

3. **Progress** – progress is the aspect of moving on. Internal questions such as, "What can I do right now to get over this and move on?" or, "What am I going to learn from this experience?" or, "In reality, how stressful is it actually?" are questions that can bring about a whole new spin on stressors.

"We don't see things as they are, we see them as we are."

Anaïs Nin

Adjust your mindset

In a nutshell, your mindset is the way you view yourself, your circumstances, and the world around you: it's the way you see things and, crucially, the way you think about things. Mindset can be split into two main categories …

Fixed mindset

With a fixed mindset, you believe that you are as you are and things are as they are and that's it! In terms of your everyday life, this means you will believe that any skills or talents you have are just "natural" abilities you happen to have been born with and the same goes for skills and talents you don't have; you believe you're stuck with your lot and nothing is going to change that.

Growth mindset

With a growth mindset, you believe that who you are now and the way things are now are *not* fixed and that everything has the potential to change. In terms of your everyday life, this means you will always see the potential to achieve more. Even with natural abilities, you'll believe that with dedicated effort, you can continue to grow and develop your skills further, and any skills you don't currently have are skills that you have the potential to acquire.

It takes a growth mindset to be able to embrace change and move towards a better life. The good news is that an individual's mindset need not be fixed; it can be changed. However, to begin the process of change, you must first accept that if you continue to do things in the same way and think about things in the same way, you will continue to get the same results.

Choose change ...

Learn to hear the "voice" of your fixed mindset – when the pressure is on, your fixed mindset voice fills your mind with thoughts of doubt, saying, "What if I can't handle this?" or, "What if it all goes wrong?"

Recognize that you always have a choice – how you interpret a challenging situation is entirely your choice; the inner voice doesn't have all the answers!

Talk back to it with a growth mindset voice – when the fixed mindset inner voice asks, "What if you fail?" learn to reply with a growth mindset voice and say, "What if I succeed?"

Take the growth mindset action – the process of learning to listen to both voices and then making your own choices will take time, but the choice of how to deal with challenges and setbacks is ultimately yours to make.

"It all depends on how we look at things, and not how they are in themselves."

Carl Gustav Jung

Learning how to see things positively doesn't mean wearing rose-tinted glasses. In fact, it means being able to see things exactly as they are but also being able to see the potential for things to change.

"Believing that your qualities are carved in stone – the fixed mindset – creates an urgency to prove yourself over and over."

Carol Dweck

Step Four

DIVIDING STRESS AND REALITY

"The secret of health for both mind and body is not to mourn for the past, worry about the future, or anticipate troubles, but to live in the present moment wisely and earnestly"

– Buddha

Look differently ... but not with your eyes

In Western culture, we seem to hold with the old perception of mind and body being two separate entities: one being physical matter and the other being a number of electrical impulses that lead to our experience of feelings and emotions. However, in traditional Chinese medicine and many other ancient Eastern healing practices, the mind and body are considered to be much more closely connected. Western attitudes are now beginning to change as ongoing scientific research continues to build our understanding of the true depth of meaning behind the much used phrase, "the mind–body connection", and studies dedicated to mind–body medicine are continuing to uncover the scientific facts behind the well known "mind over matter" phenomenon.

Many mind–body techniques have now been scientifically proven to help bring about positive health benefits and reduce or eliminate the need for medication in many cases. For example, certain techniques promote relaxation, which in turn helps to reduce muscle tension, which in turn helps to reduce pain ... and so reduce the need for medication. Clinical studies have confirmed that the symptoms commonly associated with anxiety or depression can be controlled or eradicated with mind–body techniques such as Cognitive Behavioural Therapy (CBT), allowing individuals to learn how to counteract negative patterns of thought and associated feelings with positive thoughts, thereby creating positive feelings.

Another mind–body technique known as Compassion Focused Therapy or Compassionate Mind Training (CMT) has been developed to help individuals who experience emotional difficulties connected to high levels of self-criticism and the high levels of anxiety they feel as a consequence. High levels of anxiety are known to have a detrimental effect on physical health so CMT encourages the individual to focus their attention on the need to take care of their own wellbeing. In a nutshell, CMT helps an individual to become aware of the evolutionary reactions that happen automatically in our bodies, such as the fight or flight response, and to understand that many other "automatic" reactions are the result of learned behaviours stemming way back to our childhood experiences. Through CMT and CBT, individuals are essentially encouraged to stop giving *themselves* a hard time!

According to research, there is evidence to suggest that prolonged exposure to stress or frequent "bouts" of stress can disrupt serotonin levels in the brain. Serotonin is the "feel good" hormone that generates an overall feeling of wellbeing and the research findings show that people with a tendency towards perfectionism are more susceptible to this disruption, leading to lower levels of happiness and satisfaction in life.

You have to see positives to be able to feel positive and vice versa.

 **Think**

Look at the images below: what do you see first?

Take a moment to think about the first thing you saw when you looked at the image ...

Did you see the happy faces or the sad faces?

(*Continued*)

*Did your eyes hone in on the image of a stressed person, or
the image of a happy person?*
Which expressions stood out more than the others?

Now focus on the image you saw first: on a sliding scale,
where do you see yourself by comparison at the moment?

*Are you emotionally in the same place, or are you at the
opposite end of the spectrum?*
Is the image a current representation of you, or a representation of you in the past?

 Task

Take just five minutes out of your day to look though some
old photos: notice how you look at each of the different times
in your life, and spend a few moments simply thinking about
the changes that have taken place and how *you* have changed
along the way. Now take those thoughts and turn them into
thoughts of how you can revert to the original you – the positive, motivated and energetic you.

Draw it out ...

- Draw out a picture of yourself in any way that represents the way you see yourself right now. Have some
  fun with this exercise – it's not about artistic ability, it's

simply about sketching an image that conveys how you are seeing yourself from the inside out.

- Now draw all over your sketched image with the changes needed to create an image of who you *want* to be ... feel free to make a mess! Again, it's not an art project, it's a means of recognizing the differences between the "you" you currently are, and the "you" you want to be.

This exercise is designed to help you start looking at the positives. As mentioned in previous pages, the process of re-education in terms of what you are doing begins in your understanding of how you see the world *and*, most importantly, how you see yourself.

Remember, stress is not tangible; it's not something you can pick up, and it's not something you can put in a wheelbarrow either! Stress is something you have personally created within your own mind, and it's built in layers that reflect what you have believed to be true in the past.

Draw out that image of "you" as you see yourself and *question it*.

> **Part of your stress planning is changing your view of the triggers. You must change your view of what you believed to be triggers in the past.**

Logic

Logical thinking is distorted when stress levels are high, and all logic is replaced with biased thinking and confusion – so how can you change this state? Well, the first thing is to identify how you are thinking and to realize that you are following a state that is "packaging" the situation into the best possible way for your mind to process it. For example, take a look at the following states …

> **It can't be that good** – things never happen like that for me, things always go wrong.
> **What if it doesn't work out?** – things never happen like that for me, things always go wrong.
> **It always ends in tears** – things never happen like that for me, things always go wrong.
> **I haven't been able to do that in the past** – things never happen like that for me, things always go wrong.

It doesn't feel right – things never happen like that for me, things always go wrong.

I was told I couldn't – things never happen like that for me, things always go wrong.

These types of affirmations remove all logical thinking when faced with situations that typically bring about the beginning of a stress strategy. Breaking your previous thinking habits with the following *sub*-questioning interruptions allows your mind to starting thinking in a positive way.

How is it possible? – these things can and will happen to me, because I deserve it.

If others can do it then so can I – these things can and will happen to me, because I deserve it.

Is there another way of doing it that will make it work? – these things can and will happen to me, because I deserve it.

How can I do it in the best way possible? – these things can and will happen to me, because I deserve it.

There are many more linguistically better questions you can ask; your task is to effectively change your thinking, replacing distorted and corrupt thinking with logical thinking. Ask yourself this: am I thinking in a way that creates the best representation of the situation?

Work on stressing less by seeing more …

There are many ways of seeing situations differently; your task is not to create a fake representation of a situation, but to create a version that promotes the most effective way to produce something that is motivational and beneficial.

> ... stop burying your head in the sand, face challenges head on and get a grip!

I meet so many people through my seminars and within my personal life that ask about ways they can deal with situations they have had for many years. As I see it, you wouldn't choose to keep a painful thorn in your hand for any length of time – you'd choose to remove it at the earliest opportunity – so why choose to keep hold of anything else that causes pain or discomfort?

Stress, although a labelled emotion, is something that hinders positive thinking, motivation and comfort, and therefore it should be treated in the same way you would treat an uncomfortable thorn – and indeed anything else from this point forward that fails to benefit your life in the way you deserve.

Break it down ...

Massive tasks always seem daunting at first, no matter how many times you have faced and completed similar tasks before or achieved success in other ways. However, just as a building is built brick by brick and not wall by wall, you should look to break down your barriers or stressors in the same step-by-step way. Remember, a lot of effort and energy has gone into *achieving* stress so you must now switch your focus to *ridding* yourself of stress.

Find your escapism

Just as an athlete gets into "the zone" before a race, you may have used this form of channelling in times of stress and in the initial coping situation (management). By this, I mean there may have been times in your past life in which you have just "zoned out" and experienced a sense of melting into the environment.

I remember a time when this happened to me. It was at a point in my life when everything seemed to be going to plan; I was spending time with a loved one, surrounded by rolling hills, the sun was shining and our picnic was filled with the most amazing Mediterranean foods. The kids were playing, there was a soft breeze, and the air was filled with the smell of wild flowers ... as you can imagine, it was perfect. Unfortunately it's a little far away for me to return there every time I want to take five minutes out, but by drawing on the memories and thoughts I can immediately take myself back to that place with ease and clarity. That compact moment in my past has provided a calming escape whenever I've needed it.

Find your zone ...

Creating your zone is highly personal and something that is tailored according to your emotions. It may contain music, friends, or even people no longer alive, but whichever way you achieve it, it's a mental escapism that allows your thoughts to wander and/or your body to be at rest.

As you now know, rest and recovery are essential if you are going to ask your body to perform at its peak during times of need. Remember, you can't expect a Ferrari to run on budget fuel ...

 **Think**

Spend just a few moments now to think back to a time when your body was relaxed; a time and place you can instantly return to when you close your eyes. As you do, think about how quickly your mind is able to wander ... What do you see? Who is around you? What can you sense?

Be aware of your breathing and just relax ... now you have found your zone ... create a trigger that will allow you to return to that place; some like to think of a word, others prefer a more physical, kinaesthetic approach such as squeezing their thumbs and forefinger together. Use whatever you feel works best for you and practise this a few times until you can trigger that response, that internal vision and those emotions instantly without external thoughts.

Get into a routine of using this "past life" trigger response at least once a day for the following 21 days. The more relaxed you feel on the inside, the more relaxed you will appear on the outside.

Is it real ... or imaginary?

A study carried out by a team of neuroscientists at Harvard University concluded that the human brain is unable to differentiate between what's real and what's imagined.

In the study, one group of participants were shown how to play a simple five-note tune on a piano. The tune involved moving each finger once in sequence and the same sequence was then repeated for two hours each day for five consecutive days.

A separate group of participants were taught the same five-note sequence but they were instructed to *imagine* themselves playing the notes on a piano, the notes were not actually played in reality. They also practiced playing the imaginary five-note tune for two hours each day for five consecutive days.

The brains of both groups were examined daily with the use of TMS (Transcranial Magnetic Stimulation) and scientists found there was no notable difference between the groups in terms of brain stimulation. In both groups, the brain growth resulting from the learning and repeating of the activity was the same, showing that the brain responded in the same way to both the *actual* and the *imagined* playing of the notes.

The real *mind – body connection* ...

The results of numerous scientific studies have added much weight to the belief that the human mind has the power to facilitate healing in the body. Just as imagining playing notes on a piano can stimulate the brain in the same way as actually playing the notes, imagining that your body is healing has been shown in many cases to promote *actual* healing.

It's well known in the world of elite sport that visualization techniques can aid an athlete's training by stimulating the actual muscles and neural pathways used in a movement without the need to physically perform the movement. This means that precise patterns of movement can be repeatedly practised without generating physical fatigue, thereby greatly lowering the potential for injuries to occur.

In the same way, it's possible that actual healing can take place in the body as a result of thinking about the healing process. If your thoughts are focused on how it would feel to be healed, the brain, unable to differentiate between actual healing and imagined healing, may then be stimulated to send out signals that lead to changes taking place at a cellular level and actual healing taking place as a result.

> *"The mind has exactly the same power as the hands: not merely to grasp the world, but to change it."*
>
> Colin Wilson

As explained already, your body releases stress hormones in response to situations in which you experience "stress" and it's now clear that your body responds in the same way whether the stressors are real or imagined. The hormones released affect your body both physically and emotionally and science has proven that prolonged exposure to these effects can disrupt the body's natural ability to heal itself. It's now known that certain negative mental attitudes can contribute to the onset of certain health issues such as obesity, insulin resistance, coronary heart disease, and unhealthy levels of cholesterol. However, it must be noted that there is no evidence to suggest that negative thoughts and attitudes *cause* disease, but there's a growing body of evidence that supports the link between the negative emotions and thought patterns of stress and poor physical health.

"The root of all health is in the brain. The trunk of it is in emotion. The branches and leaves are the body. The flower of health blooms when all parts work together."

Kurdish folk wisdom

Step Five

RE-ESTABLISHING A NORMAL LIFE

"Just living is not enough … one must have sunshine, freedom, and a little flower."

– Hans Christian Andersen

As Homo sapiens, we have evolved over millions of years, and over those years we have been moulded into a species that's highly dependent on everything working to systems. When you take a moment to consider the speed at which modern technology is now changing the world we live in, it's no surprise that there can be days – perhaps even longer – in which our essential needs are not being met. What this means is that our bodies are unable to keep up with the speed of technology on a day in, day out basis, so in effect we are not evolving fast enough to suit our environment. As a result, we are pushing our own internal "evolutionary" threshold, and the by-product of this is stress.

Something it's also important to consider is that within this time our diets have radically changed, not only in terms of the foods we eat but also the water we drink and the air we breathe. Do I think this has had an effect on our ability to deal/cope with stress? Yes, absolutely. Why? – For the simple reason that each and every molecule entering our body has the potential to affect our brain.

Wouldn't it be amazing to culture your own body and have control over your mental well-being?

What would you do more of?

What restrictions would be lifted and in what ways would your future bear a massive difference to your past?

What is stopping you from taking the action right now to remove those stressors from within your life?

Flip it!

Let's flip stress for a moment ...

It's very easy to look at stress as a negative simply because we have been educated in a way that drives us to think of stress in this way. However, what would happen if we were to flip stress and the internal factors and use them in a way that promotes betterment and success?

Crazy concept I know ... but wouldn't it be amazing?

Wouldn't it be amazing if all of the internal emotions, chemicals and behaviours could be used in a positive way? Wouldn't it be amazing if every time you were in an environment you would normally find stressful, you had total control over what happened and you were able to manage it just as you would manage your diary ... ?

What if we viewed stress in terms of *benefits*, not *symptoms*? By making this simple change in language patterns, the symptoms of stress become benefits and we can view stress as the release of trapped energy, and the stress reaction as the unlocking of our full superhuman potential!

In sport, not all stress is viewed as bad stress. Competitive athletes know how to use the *benefits* of the stress reaction to their advantage, making full use of the instinctive fight or flight response to make sure they're "firing on all cylinders" just when they need that superhuman boost most! Olympic athletes don't experience competitive nerves (stress) as *symptoms*; they make full use of the physiological reaction and *benefit* from its effects on their body by staying mentally in control. They *manage* stress and use it to give them the competitive "edge" they need to succeed.

The stress strategy ... making it work for you

Like most things in life, there is a beginning, middle and end, and stress is no different. In fact, it can easily be broken down into stages, and each stage is part of the overall stress strategy. There are going to be variations but the following offers a fair representation of the general path:

The Event (Stressor)
The Reading (Interpretation)
The Reaction (Behaviour)

Although simplified, when broken down in this way it makes perfect sense. The stressor, as explained earlier, you have *absolute control* over; you decide where you put yourself and you choose the behaviour you adopt. I can't make this point clearer – *no-one else has control over your emotions other than you.*

They may think they do, and they may have the ability to manipulate them, but the absolute control over your emotions is yours and yours alone.

Hard to accept, isn't it?

What else can we blame for stress ...?

Okay, this is a bit of a hard-hitting approach but I think it's an area that seems to be missed when talking about stress. Within our modern-day culture, it's very easy for us to bring out the "blame stick" and point it at anything that doesn't go our way. We can point it at number of things including:

Relationships – "I'm stressed because my partner is making demands/being needy," and so on.

Employment – "I'm stressed because I'm up against tight deadlines."

Friendship – "I'm stressed because I don't have enough time for everyone."

Modern technology – "I'm stressed because I don't have time to deal with self-serve checkouts that can't identify items in the bagging area!"

Debt – "I'm stressed because I don't know how I'm going to make ends meet."

If any of these resonate with you, or you know of any other daily situations that lead to you brandishing the "blame stick", you need to look at those situations differently ...

No-one else has control over your emotions other than you.

Start your day differently

I have found in the majority of cases, and I've experienced it for myself, when your day starts badly it continues to get a lot worse. This is a common feeling that's experienced globally – and I am certainly not the first person to point it out!

So why is this? Why does a bad start to the day tend to lead into a bad day in general? Well, your mind works to notify you of situations that offer similarity – this is because you're *looking* for negatives so it's easy to see them – and your mind is looking for similarities because you have flagged the "bad start" as an area of interest.

Think bad thoughts and get bad things.

Using competitive sport as an example once more, top-level athletes are skilled in the use of visualization techniques. They have a clear vision in their mind's eye of themselves putting in a perfect winning performance – they know what it's going to feel like; what it's going to look like, sound like, even smell and taste like – *every* detail is clear. But, and it's a big but, they have also prepared themselves mentally for *every* eventuality. For example, a 400 metre track athlete may have visualized himself running a perfect race from his favoured starting position in the middle to inside lanes, but he will also have prepared himself mentally for being drawn in the outside lane. Now, compare the "bad start" to your day and your choice to continue looking for negatives with an elite athlete's "bad start" in terms of lane draw and his ability to continue focusing on positives, and you gain a deeper understanding of the fact that *no-one else has control over your emotions other than you*. Whether or not a bad start to your day leads into a bad day is *your choice*.

The process of changing this thought process is very simple: you make a conscious *choice* to change your thinking pattern. This can be via affirmations or by listing on paper the reasons why you are going to change within that moment. This might seem overly simple, but it works, and in time it will only require a moment to switch from a negative state to a positive state.

Some sobering stats on stress to galvanize your choice to change …

According to statistics gathered by the American Psychological Association (APA), the following effects of stress are commonly experienced:

- 47 per cent of adults lie awake at night or have difficulty sleeping.
- 45 per cent of adults experience frequent feelings of anger or irritability.
- 43 per cent of adults experience fatigue.
- 40 per cent of adults experience a lack of motivation and feel a lack of interest and/or energy.
- 34 per cent of adults feel sad or depressed.
- 34 per cent of adults report having frequent headaches.
- 32 per cent of adults frequently feel that they could cry.
- 27 per cent of adults frequently experience indigestion or an upset stomach.

APA research also shows that the most commonly chosen "coping" strategies are effectively exacerbating the situation ...

- 56 per cent of women (40 per cent of men) reported making poor food choices.
- 48 per cent of men and women reported a tendency to overeat as well as eating unhealthy foods, and 39 per cent reported skipping meals in times of stress.
- 43 per cent of women and 32 per cent of men reported taking frequent naps.
- 25 per cent of women and 11 per cent of men reported using "retail therapy" and going shopping.
- 18 per cent of women and men reported using alcohol.
- 16 per cent reported using cigarettes.

Don't see a problem, resolve a problem ...

When my children come to me with a problem, I immediately ask how they are going to resolve it. I rarely ask what the problem is as the problem is unimportant – it's the resolution on which our efforts must be focused.

If you wake up in the morning, or indeed face any situation that constantly brings about negative or unhelpful states, then perhaps it's time to re-think and change the route this path follows. See the potential and not the issue; focus on what is important and avoid focusing on what is of little or no use. See all negativity as baggage, and see what can be learned from the experience as a beneficial tool.

"Happiness, like unhappiness, is a proactive choice."

Stephen Covey

Half empty or half full ... ?

Recent research has shown that those who see their glass as half full are able to manage stress in everyday life better than those who see their glass as half empty. In other words, individuals with an optimistic outlook handle stress better than individuals who tend to adopt a pessimistic outlook.

A study involved 135 adults and stress levels were measured by monitoring the amount of cortisol present in their saliva. Each participant was asked to provide information on their perceived level of stress in daily life and they were also asked to "label" themselves as being either an optimist or a pessimist in day-to-day life. This meant that researchers could then use the information to measure each individual's stress levels against their own average or "normal" levels.

"For some people, going to the grocery store on a Saturday morning can be very stressful, so that's why we asked people how often they felt stressed or overwhelmed during the day and compared people to their own averages, then analysed their responses by looking at the stress levels over many days."

Joelle Jobin, PhD

Results concluded that pessimists tended to have a lower threshold to stress compared to optimists, and they also experienced more difficulty in terms of controlling or regulating their system when going through or facing particularly stressful situations. All-in-all, the study confirms the relationship between the way we think and our ability to deal with stress. If you only ever see the glass as half empty, you set yourself on a path of seeing only the negatives in your life. With this being the case, it really is time to re-think and change the route this path follows.

"There is little difference in people, but that little difference makes a big difference. The little difference is attitude. The big difference is whether it is positive or negative."

W. Clement Stone

But I don't have time to exercise ...

If you're in the habit of seeing problems rather than solutions, then you're no doubt going to have a list of "reasons" why you're unable to fit regular exercise into your everyday life. Well, as someone who chooses to adopt a no-nonsense approach to such things, let me just say that it's time to accept that your *reasons* are nothing more than *excuses*.

Not having time to exercise is one of the most commonly used excuses for not exercising, along with not having enough energy left over at the end of the day, not having enough money to join a gym, having some form of debilitating ailment or chronic injury or just being too old.

> *"Those who think they have not time for bodily exercise will sooner or later have to find time for illness."*
>
> Edward Stanley

So, if you believe you don't have time to exercise, how much time do you believe you need – an hour, two hours, more? Well, the current guidelines provided by the government in the UK state that adults should aim to participate in 30 minutes of moderate intensity exercise per day, five days per week. In the US, the latest guidelines produced by the American College of Sports Medicine state that an adult should aim to participate in 150 minutes of moderate intensity CV (cardiovascular) activities each week, and this can be achieved in a single session of 30–60 minutes duration per day, five days per week, or in multiple shorter sessions of as little as

10 minutes in duration each time spread across the day, five days per week.

The point I really want to make is that if you were given the opportunity to take part in something that wouldn't normally be a part of your day but you *wanted* to take part in it, you'd *make* time availible to do it, wouldn't you? So, with that said, if exercise was something you *wanted* to do, you'd make time in your day to do it.

Lack of time is not the issue, it's lack of inclination!

Finding the inclination to make time for exercise becomes much easier when you gain a deeper understanding of the benefits of exercise – both physical *and* mental.

Extensive medical research has proven beyond any shadow of doubt that exercise is good for you – fact! It's well documented that an active lifestyle not only has the potential to add years to your life, but also life to your years by reducing the likelihood of developing chronic and debilitating health issues.

The proven physical benefits of exercise include:

- **A lowered risk of developing heart disease and/or suffering a stroke** – the biggest cause of death and illness in the UK is cardiovascular disease, meaning disease relating to the heart and blood vessels. Current statistics show that those living an inactive lifestyle can reduce their potential of developing life-threatening heart disease by half simply by making exercise a regular part of their day.

- **Lowered blood pressure** – if you currently have high blood pressure, regular exercise can help to lower it, thereby reducing your risk of suffering a heart attack or stroke. Exercise can also help to prevent high blood pressure from developing in the first place. This is of particular importance as high blood pressure is becoming increasingly common, but can be difficult to detect initially because it has no symptoms.

- **Improved cholesterol levels** – low levels of "good" cholesterol (HDL) and high levels of "bad" cholesterol (LDL) increase the risk of developing heart disease. Medical studies have proven that regular exercise helps to regulate cholesterol and also increase HDL levels.

- **A reduced risk of developing some types of cancer** – the results of ongoing medical research show evidence that suggests regular exercise can help to protect against breast cancer in post-menopausal women and colon cancer in all adults. There's also growing evidence to support the discovery that it may play a role in preventing lung and endometrial cancers.

- **Weight management and control** – excess body weight can cause joint and mobility problems. In addition, excess body fat increases the potential of developing high blood pressure, stroke, type 2 diabetes and heart disease, so all in all, being overweight has a negative impact on your health. We all *know* this, but statistics show that we actually double the risk of developing these health issues if we become clinically obese.

Consuming more calories than the body needs leads to the excess being stored as fat, but regular exercise helps the body to burn more calories.

The proven mental benefits of exercise include:

- **Prevention and treatment of mental health issues** – it's now medically recognized that an inactive lifestyle increases our susceptibility to develop symptoms of depression. Regular exercise is now proven to be an effective preventative measure and treatment of such symptoms, generating the same success rate as medication or talk therapy, without unwelcome side effects.

  "We now have evidence to support the claim that exercise is related to positive mental health as indicated by relief of symptoms of depression and anxiety."

  Dr Daniel Landers, Arizona State University

- **Lowered stress levels.**
- **Lowered levels of anxiety** – exercise is now medically proven to be an effective stress reliever and studies have also proven its effectiveness in alleviating the symptoms of panic attacks, phobias and other anxiety-related disorders.
- **Improved sleep patterns.**
- **Improved self-esteem and confidence.**
- **Increased sense of overall happiness and wellbeing.**
- **The potential for improved brain function!**

The proven benefits of exercise should be enough to motivate you to change the way you think about exercise, and to encourage you to find the time to include regular exercise in your life. So, the next question must be – what is the meaning of "moderate intensity" exercise? In the UK, the NHS defines exercise intensity in the following way:

Light – at this intensity you are able to carry on a conversation as you exercise.
Moderate – at this intensity you become slightly breathless.
Vigorous – at this intensity you begin to breathe rapidly.

In more detail, the guidelines define moderate intensity exercise as " ... working hard enough to raise your heart rate and break a sweat". However, a popular way of assessing whether or not you're exercising at the most beneficial intensity is to sing a song as you exercise. At a light intensity, you're able to sing the lyrics without any difficulty, but at a moderate intensity, you're unable to finish longer sentences without taking a breath. At a vigorous intensity, you become unable to gasp out more than two or three words between breaths. The intensity of your exercise session is your choice, and it's worth noting that 75 minutes of vigorous intensity exercise each week generates the same level of benefits as 150 minutes of moderate intensity exercise each week.

It must also be noted that one person's definition of "moderate intensity" is not necessarily the same as the next person's. For example, what constitutes *moderate* for Usain Bolt probably constitutes beyond *vigorous* for most of the general population!

Fitness professionals working in a gym environment often use a simple but effective method of determining the correct level of intensity for each client known as the Borg PRE scale, ranging from 6 (no exertion at all) to 20 (maximal exertion). The scale helps to identify the exerciser's rate of perceived exertion, making it possible to then tailor each individual's exercise programme to ensure they work out at the most beneficial level of intensity on each piece of exercise equipment.

Because the official Borg Scale of RPE uses a sliding scale ranging from 6 to 20, many variations of the scale are now in use with a simpler 1 to 10 numbering system in place instead. It can be helpful to use your own words to describe how each level makes you feel so that you can easily bring to mind the way you should be feeling as you exercise in order to gain the maximum benefits from each session. For example, in your customised RPE scale, a level of 1–2 becomes "no exertion at all" and 3–4 becomes "extremely light" but you might choose to define a level of 1–2 as sitting on your couch watching TV, and a level of 3–4 as taking a leisurely walk around town doing some window shopping. When using a 1–10 scale, a level of 5–7 equates to moderate intensity exercise and a level of 7–8 equates to vigorous intensity, with anything above level 8 only being used in very short bursts of effort with lower intensity recovery periods in between.

Finding time to exercise is not about having to "give up" time, it's about making better use of the time you have.

 Task

Read through the benefits of exercise listed earlier once more and *commit* to making time for exercise. Be realistic and keep in mind that radical or extreme changes are unlikely to be lasting changes. Begin as you mean to go on and commit to a *dedicated* time slot for exercise. In the grand scale of things it doesn't matter whether you choose to commit to a one hour slot once a week or a 10 minute slot once a day initially; all that matters is that you commit to exercising on a regular basis so that you begin to develop an "exercise habit".

Mark it in your diary ...

It's often said that a new habit can be established (or an established habit broken) within 21 days of concentrated effort, but further research in this area has revealed that it takes closer to 60 days to make a new pattern of behaviour or new routine feel established to the point of becoming a habit, or "easier to do than not to do". So, look at your diary and mark each exercise session you're committing to for the next 60 days. Write it down and commit to doing it – no excuses!

"There are only two options regarding commitment. You're either in or you're out. There's no such thing as life in-between."

Pat Riley

Step Six

CREATING A LASTING RHYTHM

"Happiness is not a matter of intensity but of balance, order, rhythm and harmony."

– Thomas Merton

Now is a good time to revisit the physical and emotional effects of stress on your body and to use your understanding to galvanize your determination to *stress less* and to begin achieving what in the past felt unachievable.

You should be aware of cognitive symptoms of stress, which include memory problems, inability to concentrate, poor judgment, seeing only the negative, anxious or racing thoughts and constant worrying. When you are stressed you may experience emotional symptoms such as moodiness, irritability or short temper, agitation, inability to relax, feeling overwhelmed, feeling a sense of loneliness and isolation, depression or general unhappiness. You may also experience the physical symptoms like aches and pains, diarrhoea or constipation, nausea, dizziness, chest pain, rapid heartbeat, loss of sex drive or frequent colds. And be aware that stress can also lead to behavioural symptoms such as eating more or less, sleeping too much or too little, isolating yourself from others, procrastinating or neglecting responsibilities, using alcohol, cigarettes or drugs to relax, or nervous habits, for example, nail biting or pacing.

The internal stress reaction

When you perceive a threat, your nervous system responds by releasing a flood of stress hormones, including adrenaline and cortisol. These hormones rouse the body for emergency action – your heart pounds faster, muscles tighten, blood pressure rises, breathing rate quickens and your senses become sharper. These physical changes increase your strength and stamina, speed up your reaction time and enhance your focus, thereby preparing you to fight for your life or take flight from the danger at hand.

The stress reaction affects different people in different ways but the most common responses can be described as follows:

Foot on the gas – this describes an angry or agitated stress response. If this happens to you, you become heated or keyed up, overly emotional and unable to sit still.

Foot on the brake – this describes a withdrawn or depressed stress response. If this happens to you, you shut down, space out and show very little energy or emotion.

Foot on both – this describes a tense and frozen stress response. If this happens to you, you "freeze" under pressure and can't do anything. You look paralysed but under the surface you're extremely agitated.

You *are* what you eat!

This might seem like a worn-out old mantra from the 1960s but believe me, the foods you eat have a massive effect on your overall ability to make positive and supporting judgements. Food offers the very key ingredients you need to make a positive and lasting lifestyle change, and it plays a much bigger role in eliminating stress than most would assume.

"Tell me what you eat, and I will tell you what you are."

Anthelme Brillat-Savarin

We all know what it feels like after a night of indulgence; the brain fails to function correctly and generally everything feels clouded; your reactions are lengthened and the smallest of tasks can take three times the amount of time. Why do this? ... Who knows! It would seem in our society that we enjoy putting pressure on our mind and body and then we reward it by doing completely the opposite.

My story ...

During 2012, I decided to make a study of the effect food could have on the mind. After completing my sports nutrition and personal training course in 2010, I realized that the more I looked into foods and nutritional needs in sports, the more I learned about the connection between the body's performance – both physical and mental – and the quality and intake of fuel in the form of food. Using myself as the guinea pig, I researched the effects of a range of products on my body and my thinking – both good and bad – including my response to stress and my stress threshold. As a result, I'm now able to use my experience to draw a good, educated conclusion.

Conclusion: the more quality food you eat the better your life will become.

Okay, my conclusion may seem like I'm stating the obvious, but if it's so obvious, why are so few of us doing it? You see, we all *know* that sugary foods and processed meals are not good for us and not nearly as healthy as those made using raw ingredients, yet we still convince ourselves that eating those unhealthy foods is okay.

The point I want to make here is that stress can largely be attributed to failing to provide your body with the nutrients it has evolved to *need*.

> *"Let food be thy medicine and medicine be thy food."*
>
> Hippocrates

The stress and weight gain

It's well known that times of stress can lead to making poor food choices and reaching for so-called "comfort foods" that are generally high in fat, sugar and salt. It's also well known that these foods are responsible for unhealthy weight gain, and this has led to weight gain and obesity being associated with stress. However, it's now also known that individuals maintaining a healthy diet can still experience unhealthy weight gain as a result of stress and that the associated gains in abdominal fat increase the risk of developing heart problems and diabetes.

The increase in abdominal fat is now believed to be the result of increased levels of cortisol (the stress hormone) in the body. Cortisol (in conjunction with other glucocorticoid hormones) has been found to play a role in the food cravings and "comfort eating" associated with stress, and evidence suggests that this may help to lower the negative impact of stress on the body. For example, carbohydrates have been shown to increase the production of serotonin (the feel-good hormone), which generates an overall improvement in mood. Interestingly, overeating appears to be triggered by different stressors in women compared to men, with women tending to comfort eat in response to family and relationship-related issues, and men in response to work-related issues such as a lack of control in the decision-making process or pressures surrounding the learning of new skills. However, both men and women overeat in response to financial difficulties.

Bonetti's SFSL

The SFSL is short for STRESS FREE SHOPPING LIST ...

Although meaning nothing outside the boundaries of this book, this list has helped many of my clients and it's something I'm able to share with them in the hope that they will improve their overall lifestyle and reverse or lessen the effects of toxins within the mind. Of course, the SFSL is only as effective as the person implementing it – reading it changes nothing, you have to *apply* it! However, for those committed to change, it provides a guide in terms of demonstrating how easy it is to combine healthy ingredients with a little creativity to create an *enjoyable* healthy eating and lifestyle plan.

If you're as passionate as I am about getting more from your mind and body, then look to incorporate the following ingredients into your current shopping list, or better still, use them as stand-alone replacements for your usual ingredients:

Wholefoods – choose whole grains, lentils, beans, nuts/ seeds and vegetables. Take advantage of darker green vegetables such as broccoli and spinach, and root vegetables such as yams and sweet potatoes.

Fruits – use fruits in moderation, avoiding high GI fruits such as bananas. Select fruits such as apples and berries, and use these in smoothies as well as enjoying them raw.

GI = Glycemic Index

The glycemic index is a measure of how fast a food raises your blood glucose (sugar) levels and by how much. The higher the GI value (out of a top value of 100), the more rapidly the food raises your blood glucose levels. Glucose is the body's primary source of fuel, so eating foods with a lower GI value (lower than 50) helps to provide your body with a steadier supply of energy spread over a longer period of time compared to the sugar "spikes" created by high GI foods. As an example, ripe bananas can have a GI value as high as 58 whereas cherries have a GI of 22 and raspberries or strawberries typically have a GI value of around 30.

10 a day – our current "5 a day" food guidelines in relation to fruits and vegetables should be increased to 10 a day, meaning you should aim to consume a wide variety of different fruits and vegetables throughout the course of each day to ensure you are meeting your body's minimum macronutrient needs.

Go RAW – keep away from sugars and all forms of processed foods; this means steering clear of anything that has been refined using bleached sugars and, even more importantly, anything containing sugar replacements.

If you can't pronounce the ingredients, the likelihood is that you shouldn't be eating it.

Quality Protein – there are many useful online resources to help you calculate your optimum protein intake, however, in my experience, you should aim for a daily food intake of 40 per cent protein, 30 per cent carbohydrates and 30 per cent fats – but more on this later.

Your mind, once drained of water, is about 70 per cent fat ...

Healthy Fats – omegas -3, -6 and -9 have a much more important role to play in a healthy diet than we are led to believe. They boost immunity, decrease inflammation and pain, and help the body to control and regulate insulin, which is essential for establishing a stable and working sugar balance. They also have a key role within the workings of the brain and the performance of the neurotransmitters, and this has been proven to reduce the effects of stress, depression and schizophrenia.

Look after your neurotransmitters ...

Just as looking after a car by keeping it well oiled and serviced regularly helps to increase its longevity and keep it running smoothly, looking after your neurotransmitters by providing your brain with the nutrients it needs has a similar effect on the "mechanics" of your mind. There are many different types of neurotransmitters (the bits that relay information) but they can be categorized into the following key areas:

- **Adrenaline** (epinephrine) **noradrenaline, dopamine** – these are produced by the adrenal glands as part of the body's stress response. Collectively they increase your heart rate and breathing to increase the flow of blood to your muscles as part of the "fight or flight" response, but they also create the "high" experienced by runners or the "buzz" craved by "adrenaline junkies" who take part in extreme sports!

- **GABA** – in a nutshell, GABA (gamma-aminobutyric-acid) calms excited nerve impulses, so they have a calming effect, working to reverse the effects of the "high" created by adrenaline, and a deficiency can result in symptoms of anxiety and nervousness.

- **Serotonin** – often referred to as the "happy hormone", serotonin helps to generate a general feeling of wellbeing by regulating your mood and keeping a lid on anxiety. It's also known to help relieve symptoms of depression and/or aggression, and it's a natural sleep aid.

- **Acetylcholine** – this is the main neurotransmitter involved in learning, thought and memory. It keeps your memory and mind actively responsive, sharpening your perception and concentration, so it's responsible for alerting you to potential dangers and triggering a fast reaction.

So why are these so important? Well, as mentioned previously, your body is a vehicle; the more you service and maintain it the better it will perform, but if you leave it to rust ... well, that's exactly what will happen.

Important note: Accept that you must keep your body refreshed with essential vitamins and minerals to ensure it runs smoothly.

Brain foods

Were you ever told as a child to eat fish because it would make you "brainy"? Well, there's a lot of truth in that statement. Brain foods are anything that produces naturally occurring omega fats. Oily fish such as salmon, mackerel, sardines, tuna and anchovies are proven "brain foods" along with kelp, eggs, walnuts and linseed, pumpkin, sunflower and sesame seeds. The fact that walnuts have a brain-like appearance is perhaps nature's quirky way of pointing us in the right direction! Many of these key brain foods can easily become part of your daily diet, perhaps adding seeds to your morning breakfast cereal or potting a few walnuts to enjoy as a mid-afternoon snack.

Stress-busting nutrition!

When under the additional pressures of stress, the nutritional needs of your body change. Under normal circumstances, the B vitamins play a vital role in helping to convert protein, carbohydrates and fats into energy. In times of stress, there is an increased need for the presence of these vitamins in the diet to help keep things functioning as they should. For this reason, vitamin B5 is often referred to as the "anti-stress vitamin" as it has an essential role to play in maintaining the proper functioning of the adrenal glands, thereby helping the body to cope with stress. Another key vitamin in the functioning of the adrenal glands is vitamin C, so the increased demands created by the stress reaction can lead to supplies quickly becoming depleted.

> **B vitamins** – good sources are liver and brewer's yeast.
> **Vitamin B5** – good sources are avocado and mushrooms.
> **Vitamin C** – good sources are blackcurrants, papaya, mango and green peppers.

Certain minerals also play an important role in stress-busting nutrition:

> **Potassium** – extra potassium is needed as the extra stress placed on the body causes an increase in energy

production, which in turn causes an increase in the levels of potassium being excreted. This must be replaced, as it is needed for healthy nerve cell function.

Good sources are dark green leafy vegetables, mushrooms and beans such as kidney beans.

Magnesium – this mineral plays a role in ensuring efficient nerve transmission but as with potassium, periods of stress can lead to supplies becoming depleted. Low levels of magnesium can result in mental confusion and fatigue, and may lead to insomnia.

Good sources are green leafy vegetables.

Calcium – this mineral works together with magnesium to help maintain healthy nerve function; it also plays a role in helping to combat insomnia and symptoms of irritability.

Good sources are dairy products and green leafy vegetables.

A note about lecithin: lecithin is a fat found in foods such as egg yolks, soya beans and liver. It also plays an important role in the body, helping with the transmission of nerve impulses in the cells. To manufacture the neurotransmitter acetylcholine your body needs choline, which is a component of lecithin, and this has led to it often being referred to as "nerve food". It is used in the treatment of dementia, Alzheimer's disease and other memory disorders, and studies have also proven its effectiveness in the treatment of anxiety and certain forms of depression.

When your body is subjected to prolonged periods of stress it can quickly become deficient in the previously listed vitamins and minerals, which will mean your nervous system is no longer able to function efficiently. It's also known that under the extra pressures of the stress reaction, the body digests and absorbs food much less efficiently, which means that replacing the key nutrients becomes difficult. This generates a Catch-22 … when under stress your body is in need of the stress-busting nutrients, but getting them is being made more difficult by the effects of the stress reaction!

Mood food

It's well known that in times of stress or when you're feeling low, certain "comfort foods" become much more appealing. These foods include chocolate and sugary treats, coffee or drinks containing caffeine, alcohol, and nicotine in the case of smokers. However, contrary to the popular belief that these foods make you feel better, in reality they actually make things worse. For a start, alcohol and nicotine add to the workload on your already under pressure adrenal glands, and they're probably going to disrupt your sleep – and a lack of sleep can only add to the pressure your body is under. Many people believe that alcohol "calms" them down at the end of a stressful day but studies have shown that a dependency on alcohol makes a person four times more likely to develop an anxiety disorder than a non-drinker or less frequent drinker. Caffeine, as we all know, can also disrupt normal sleep patterns and in some people it is known to induce a state of anxiety, sometimes leading to panic attacks, along with increased irritability and an increased potential to suffer from depression.

 Task

Remove all stimulants ...

Over the next week, begin to remove all of the simulants presently in your daily diet and considered part of your everyday rituals. I remember going through this process and how difficult it was, but I made a conscious effort to continue by accepting that the difficulties I faced were simply a reminder of just how dependent I actually was. These stimulants have a negative effect on your body, playing havoc with the natural production and distribution of hormones.

We have all experienced times when we've felt tired and consumed a coffee or caffeine supplement as a "pick me up" only to feel the crash effects a matter of hours later. This can lead into a vicious cycle of continued use, but it's this pattern of abuse that leads into dependency.

Do you need a coffee to kick start your day?
Do you drink an energy drink just before working out?

Over the coming weeks, start to wean yourself off these supplements. Allow your body to return to its normal production levels and keep a record of the change in emotions you experience and any changes in the way your body feels as a result of the lack of these products in your system.

My story ...

When I weaned myself off dairy, I felt sick for a week, had eight days of headaches and became spotty as a result of all the toxins leaving the body. I felt fantastic from the tenth day and never looked back.

It's worth noting that this is not going to be an easy process, but, when you have eliminated dependency you can make a *choice* over whether or not you want to re-introduce each product back into your diet. I now have a cup of fresh coffee every morning before my workout and I really enjoy the whole process from grinding the beans to the taste. As a point of interest, it is said that 100 mg of caffeine a day is all it takes to produce an addictive (habitual) need.

Important note: Accept from this point forwards that your body needs more natural nutrients to produce its own vital chemicals naturally and less unnatural nutrients provided by unnaturally produced and chemically manufactured foods and drinks!

Steer clear of junk foods – they provide nothing more than empty calories; they use up valuable nutrients in the process of being digested; they cause an unhealthy imbalance in blood sugar levels, and they can lead to symptoms of anxiety, irritability and depression.

Don't forget!

When you take all of this into consideration, it's clear that the human body has an amazing capacity to protect itself from illness and to pre-empt issues that are likely to arise. However, it needs good fuel to be able to keep performing at its best. With this in mind, do you become more forgetful when you are stressed?

It's now known that raised cortisol levels over an extended period of time can significantly increase memory loss. Cortisol, more commonly known as the "stress hormone", is secreted into the bloodstream as part of the stress response and while this is perfectly normal, it must be remembered that the stress response was designed for immediate and temporary use, and not for the lengthy periods of time we're now expecting our bodies to continue coping with it. Studies have shown that raised cortisol levels not only have a negative effect on the present functioning of your body, it can also have a damaging and lasting effect on memory function.

The stress – memory loss connection

Scientific research has proven that stress has an effect on the brain – memory functions in particular – but the level of effect is dependent upon whether acute or chronic stress is experienced.

Acute stress – studies have shown that acute stress leads to an overall heightening of your senses, including an increase in concentration levels to help you deal with the imminent threat or danger, but your short-term memory and your verbal memory in particular is impaired, hence the "speechlessness" often experienced during moments of acute stress.

Chronic stress – studies have shown that chronic stress leads to a decrease in concentration levels, which has a detrimental effect on your work performance and your ability to learn, and it can also lead to becoming more accident-prone. Long-term exposure to stressors increases cortisol levels in the body and this is now linked to evidence of shrinking in the area of the brain responsible for memory. Ongoing studies have yet to determine whether the effects of shrinking can be reversed.

A note on **DHEA**: Dehydroepiandrosterone (DHEA) is a naturally occurring chemical in the body that helps to regulate stress levels and maintain an equal balance of hormones. However, as with many other natural elements of the body, the manufacturing process begins to slow down as you age. For this reason, DHEA is a popular food supplement and is commonly referred to as being the "fountain of youth" due to its potential ability to slow down the effects of ageing on the body, including the maintenance and improvement of memory functions.

If it is your aim in life is to create something fulfilling while creating abundance, then you must change your thinking, behaviour and *eating* patterns to allow your body to perform at its absolute best.

Think

Ask yourself this: what is more important – creating a lifestyle focused around natural living, or a lifestyle supported by supplements and ailments?

"A man's health can be judged by which he takes two at a time – pills or stairs."

Joan Welsh

Eat what you want

Just as finding time for exercise is something that becomes easy the moment you choose to think of exercise as something you *want* to do rather than something to be avoided, finding ways to incorporate healthier foods into your daily diet becomes easy the moment you choose to think of healthier options as the foods you *want* to eat.

If you're someone who has a list of "reasons" for not exercising, it's more than likely that you also have a list of "reasons" for not eating healthily! As you know, your *reasons* are nothing more than *excuses* and just as a lack of time is no excuse for not exercising, a lack of time is no excuse for choosing "fast food" or "convenience food" over home-cooked food prepared with natural ingredients. In reality, eating healthily is no more time consuming than eating unhealthily, and taking a "packed lunch" of home-prepared food with you to work is much faster and more convenient than having to join the queue in a fast food takeaway.

Other commonly used excuses include ...

"**Health foods" are too expensive** – a healthy, balanced diet and so-called "health foods" are not necessarily one and the same. You don't need to visit an expensive store to buy an apple or some oatmeal for example, and a bag of crisps is much more expensive than an orange or even the average cost of a bowl of nutritious and delicious homemade soup.

Healthy foods are boring – foods that are good for you offer a whole world of different tastes, and you can't get any more flavoursome than fresh, raw ingredients. All it takes is a little experimentation with herbs and spices in place of artificial flavours, salt and sugar, and you'll soon discover that along with good wholesome food comes good wholesome flavour.

Food for thought ...

All it takes to begin realizing the many benefits of a healthy diet is a change in the way you think about food. If you want to feel alive and vibrant from the moment you wake up in the morning and you want to feel energized and ready to face whatever your day brings, you need to provide your body with good quality, high-octane fuel. Think about it for a moment; attempting to fuel your body and mind with junk food is like trying to fuel a Formula 1 race car on chip fat. Home-cooked, healthy meals are not bland and boring, they needn't be expensive *and* you don't even need to be able to cook to get the most from fresh produce.

Go green!

Most of us are familiar with the idea of whizzing up some fruit along with milk or a variety of alternatives to create a nutritious shake, also known as a smoothie. The main ingredient in most smoothies is fruit but by adding vegetables to the mix using a 60 per cent fruit to 40 per cent vegetable ratio, you create an even more nutrient-dense smoothie known as a "green smoothie". A green smoothie is a great way to begin realizing the benefits of eating fresh, natural foods without having to master any cookery skills whatsoever.

Fruits that work well as smoothie ingredients include:

- **Blueberries** – these berries are considered by many to be the ultimate "brain food" due to their antioxidant properties, which can be as much as five times higher than other fruits and vegetables. According to medical research, a serving of just 100 grams each day can help to slow down the onset of issues normally associated with mental ageing by stimulating the continuation of new cell growth in the brain.

- **Strawberries** – these add a deliciously fresh and sweet flavour but they are also rich in vitamin C, which is an important antioxidant, and they play a role in helping the body to absorb the iron that's present in vegetables.
- **Pears** – these also provide a good source of vitamin C and bioflavonoids (antioxidants) along with potassium, which plays a key role in regulating your heart rate, and pectin, which provides fibre.
- **Mangoes** – another useful source of vitamin C and beta-carotene, which is the plant form of vitamin A. Vitamin A also plays a role in protecting the body against free radicals.
- **Kiwi fruit** – this flavoursome fruit is another good source of vitamin C and potassium.
- **Bananas** – these provide a "creamy" texture and they are also rich in potassium.
- **Cherries** – these provide a delicious flavour, along with potassium and vitamin C.
- **Apricots** – like mangoes, these are rich in vitamin C and beta-carotene.

Most orange or dark yellow-fleshed fruits contain beta-carotene and most red-fleshed fruits contain lycopene. It's now known that a beta-carotene and lycopene combination in the diet provides an effective means of protection from potentially damaging free radicals, although the full benefits of antioxidants are yet to be scientifically proven.

A note about free radicals and antioxidants: free radicals are a natural by-product of metabolism and they may be produced by the body to help neutralize certain bacteria. However, they are unstable cells and overproduction can be harmful. Environmental factors such as pollution, cigarette smoke, herbicides and radiation can lead to overproduction and without the aid of antioxidants, the body can struggle to manage the situation; this is when cell damage can occur. Antioxidants help to prevent cell damage and thereby they help to protect the body from disease.

Vegetables that work well as green smoothie ingredients include:

- **Spinach** – like many of the fruits mentioned previously, spinach contains vitamin C and potassium. It's also a rich source of carotenoids, which are powerful antioxidants.
- **Cabbage** – this is another rich source of vitamin C and also vitamin E, another powerful antioxidant, as well as potassium and beta-carotene. It also provides vitamin K, which plays an essential role in the formation of many proteins.
- **Broccoli** – this provides vitamin C, beta-carotene, potassium and iron – an essential mineral that helps to transport oxygen around the body in your blood, and it's also a good source of potassium, bioflavonoids and other antioxidants.
- **Collard Greens** – these provide omega-3 essential fatty acids, which have anti-inflammatory properties.
- **Pumpkin** – like banana, this can provide a "creamy" texture and it's also a good source of vitamin E and beta-carotene. The seeds are also a rich source of iron, potassium, phosphorus, magnesium and zinc,

which collectively have roles to play in hormone balance, keeping bones strong, boosting relaxation, aiding restful sleep and helping to regulate the immune system.

- **Kale** – another good source of vitamin C, beta-carotene, iron and also calcium.

A great way to boost the nutritional benefits of a green smoothie, along with giving flavours a twist, is to add fresh herbs. Good choices include:

- **Parsley** – as well as adding flavour, a sprig of parsley also provides vitamin C, beta-carotene, iron, potassium, magnesium, phosphorus, zinc, calcium and copper. Interestingly, two grams of protein can be sourced in just one cup of parsley.
- **Sorrel** – this provides iron, magnesium and calcium.
- **Dill** – this provides vitamin C, beta-carotene, iron, manganese and calcium, and also gives a sweet flavour.
- **Basil** – this also provides beta-carotene, iron and manganese, along with copper, magnesium and potassium.
- **Coriander** – this herb contains anti-inflammatory properties along with vitamin C, iron and magnesium. It gives a green smoothie a mild, peppery flavour.

Further nutrients and flavours can be added with the following:

- **Honey** – provides instant energy (glucose) and sweetness.
- **Maple Syrup or Agave Syrup** – a source of zinc and manganese as well as added sweetness.

- **Tea** – in moderation, the addition of tea helps to boost the antioxidant content.
- **Chocolate** – good quality chocolate containing over 50 per cent cocoa solids provides potassium, iron and magnesium.

There's essentially no limit to the potential fruit and vegetable combinations you might try; it all comes down to personal taste, but as the long list of possible ingredients shows, you don't need to be a cook to enjoy the benefits of fresh produce, all you need is a blender.

Here are some flavoursome green smoothie combinations to try:

Spinach with bananas, strawberries and peach – the sweetness of the fruit overrides the flavour of the spinach, providing an antioxidant-rich smoothie.

Kale with oranges and kiwi fruit – kale contains iron, calcium, vitamin C and beta-carotene, with citrus fruits also providing a rich source of vitamin C and antioxidants.

Collard greens with banana, apple, pear and dates – collard greens contain omega-3 fatty acids, thereby providing anti-inflammatory properties, and dates are good source of iron and calcium.

I have, however, come across a few individuals who were so averse to "cooking" at home that even blending a few fruits and vegetables together was considered "too much effort". If this resonates with you, consider the following steps you can take towards changing the way you eat and the way you think about food ...

Fresh is best – whenever possible, leave packaged varieties of foods on the shelf and opt for fresh varieties instead. The closer a food stays to its natural state, the greater its food value is likely to be.

Read labels – all too often, packaged foods are chosen *because* of the way they are packaged and the way they look. However, take a moment to read the "this product contains" list before putting it in your shopping trolley. Ingredients/contents lists can be lengthy and the language used difficult to decipher so for this reason, a simple rule of thumb is to limit your choices to products containing no more than six ingredients. Keep in mind that ingredients are listed in order of volume so the items at the top of the list are present in greater amounts than those at the bottom. If salt and sugar are at the top, put it back on the shelf, and the same applies if the ingredients have names you can't pronounce.

Cook your own "convenience" foods – with just a little willingness to experiment, you will soon discover that many convenience foods, which take 10 minutes to cook in the microwave, could be cooked from scratch using fresh ingredients in around the same amount of time. This is not only a step towards knowing exactly what you're eating; it's also a great way to avoid preservatives and other unnatural ingredients such as artificial colours.

Make your own "fast food" – it takes very little effort to learn how to make good food, fast. When you make the choice to improve your diet and to give your mind and body the essential nutrients needed for health and vitality, you then begin to clear your fridge and kitchen cupboards of foods that represent the opposite.

By keeping stocks of the foods your body needs and the foods you now *want* to eat readily available, you have instant access to your very own healthful, convenient, and fast meals.

Never shop hungry – if you've ever gone food shopping on an empty stomach you'll know that the temptation to fill your trolley with foods that represent instant gratification – cakes, pastries, bags of crisps and so on – can be overwhelming. Always eat a satisfying meal or snack before you shop and you'll find that you no longer have any interest in foods that do not represent healthful choices.

Food choices made easy ...

If you really do tend to do a "trolley dash" when you go food shopping, a simple way to begin making better food choices "on the run" is to use the USDA (United States Department of Agriculture) **"Go, Slow, and Whoa"** system of putting everyday foods into user-friendly categories.

GO foods – this category contains the foods that are highest in nutrients, lowest in fat and added sugar, and relatively low in calories. GO foods are the foods to enjoy almost anytime and they include fruits and vegetables, frozen and canned (without added salt or sugar) as well as fresh, whole grains, fat-free or low-fat milk products, lean meat, poultry, fish, beans, egg whites or egg substitute.

SLOW Foods – this category contains foods that have a higher added sugar and fat content than GO foods, making them higher in calories. For this reason, they should be enjoyed less frequently than GO foods. Examples include white refined flour bread, low-fat mayonnaise and semi-skimmed milk.

WHOA Foods – this category contains the foods that are highest in fat and/or added sugar. They are calorie dense but frequently low in nutritional value so WHOA foods should only be enjoyed once in a while or as a special treat. They include whole milk, cheese, butter, creamy salad dressings, fried foods, muffins, cakes and pastries.

Can't cook won't cook

Even fast food fans and die-hard non-cooks can be encouraged to make healthier food choices. A typical fast food "meal" of burger, fries and a shake contains over 1300 calories, and an alarming 45 per cent of those are fat calories. In general, fast foods also lack fibre and vitamins and contain high levels of salt. It might be possible to locate a vitamin or two at the salad bar but very often the food has been exposed to the air, light and heat for a lengthy period of time, making any real nutritional value unlikely. Of course, adding a dressing to your salad can actually add another 400 calories to your meal and with a typical burger and fries portion containing as much as 1100 mg of salt – around half of the recommended daily amount – it can make "healthy" fast food seem like an impossible dream. However, it can be done with a little creativity ...

Order an extra bun with your burger

Throw away the fat laden lower half of the bun (where the grease from the burger has soaked in!) and replace it with a fresh half. Eat the remaining fresh half as a way of boosting the reasonably healthy carbohydrate content of your meal.

Remove the skin from chicken pieces

Enjoy the meat without any skin or outer coating and order an extra bread roll if you're feeling hungry and need to bulk up your meal.

Choose grilled fish in place of deep-fried fish

And chips or fries can be substituted with bread and a side order of mushy peas!

Load up at the salad bar

Provided the salad looks reasonably fresh, take advantage of the usual "all you can eat" arrangement. A good choice might be to order a baked potato with a vegetarian chilli and then fill up your plate at the salad bar *without* adding any dressings.

Choose your pizza toppings carefully

Vegetable toppings such as peppers, mushrooms or sweetcorn make a healthier choice than extra cheese, pepperoni or sausage. Garlic bread is laden with unhealthy fat but a bread roll makes a good substitute.

Avoid creamy baked potato fillings

Choose fillings such as chilli, baked beans, ratatouille, lean ham or anything mixed with yoghurt instead of cream cheese.

Avoid mayonnaise in sandwiches

Replace mayo or other creamy sandwich fillings with juicy tomato or cucumber instead.

Remember the wise old saying, "A little of what you fancy does you good", and accept that it's really all about moderation.

You *can* cook

If you really think you can't cook, consider the simplicity of making a pot of nutrient-packed and delicious soup. A healthy, wholesome bowl of soup provides a meal in itself and it's one of the most effective ways to pack a whole host of highly nutritious foods into one meal. What makes a good, flavoursome soup is really a matter of personal taste but it's better to use three or four ingredients that you know complement each other well than to use a dozen or more just because you know they're healthy ingredients. However, there are a number of so-called "superfoods" that lend themselves ideally to the soup making process. There's no absolute definition of a superfood and there's no definitive list, but the term is used to describe the nutrient-packed foods thought to possess health-giving properties.

"An old-fashioned vegetable soup, without any enhancement, is a more powerful anti-carcinogen than any known medicine."

James Duke MD

Soup super foods!

Green leafy vegetables – choices such as kale, bok choy, spinach, Swiss chard, dandelion, mustard greens and collard greens provide high nutrition at a very low cost. They are packed with essential vitamins, minerals and health-boosting enzymes.

Herbs and spices – choices such as oregano, cilantro, parsley, thyme, peppermint, turmeric, sage and ginger have properties that can give your body a healthful boost in many ways, including giving your memory a boost.

Vegetables – these include choices such as broccoli, cabbage, cauliflower, carrots, asparagus, beets, onion and garlic. Broccoli has twice as much protein as beef, one cup of cauliflower provides a daily vitamin C requirement, and garlic has well known anti-inflammatory and antiviral benefits, and has only been shown to play a role in fighting coronary heart disease.

Whole grains and beans – choices such as brown rice, oats, quinoa, buckwheat, millet and beans provide protein and fibre. Quinoa is an excellent protein-rich food and a good source of iron, B vitamins and potassium.

Seaweeds – varieties include kelp, nori, kombu, arame, wakame and chlorella, and they are all packed with vitamins. Chlorella is nature's top energy food providing all of the essential amino acids, and miso soup made with kombu is a powerful natural remedy to a great many health issues.

"Do you have a kinder, more adaptable friend in the food world than soup?

Who soothes you when you are ill? Who refuses to leave you when you are impoverished and stretches its resources to give a hearty sustenance and cheer? You don't catch steak hanging around when you're poor and sick do you?"

Judith Martin (aka Miss Manners)

 **Task**

Commit to getting into your kitchen and making yourself a hearty pot of soup. All it takes is a change in the way you think about healthy foods and cooking ... it's easier than you *think*.

1. Make a basic soup stock using whatever vegetables you like. Roughly chop some vegetables such as parsnip, carrot, leek, onion, broccoli or celery and cover them with water in a pan. Bring to the boil, add seasoning of your choice, cover and simmer for around 30 minutes. Strain the liquid into a bowl and there you have it, vegetable stock. It's a good idea to make a larger quantity of stock than you need, then freeze the remainder ready for whenever you need it next.

2. Use your vegetable stock as your soup base and begin to add ingredients to increase the nutritional content. The health benefits provided by herbs and spices are quite remarkable. By adding your favourites to your soup you'll be boosting more than just the flavour. Experiment with pepper, basil, oregano, parsley, thyme or ginger, or any others that suit your taste.

3. Add vegetables to increase the fibre, vitamin and mineral content. Frozen vegetables can be useful alternatives when fresh produce is unavailable or out of season. Spinach, broccoli, carrots, celery, corn or

(Continued)

151

potatoes work well in most soups but use what you have available and whatever suits your taste.

4. Beans and whole grains provide more fibre and protein. They also make a soup more satisfying and create the "meal in itself" effect. Lentils, brown rice, barley, lima beans or wholewheat pasta are all good choices for soups.

5. If your soup requires a "creamy" texture, cream of tomato or cream of mushroom for example, use skimmed milk, non-fat dry milk powder or soymilk instead of whole milk or cream. This way you add calcium and protein without adding extra fat.

6. Enjoy!

Step Seven
STRESS FREE LIVING

"Life is not a matter of having good cards, but of playing a poor hand well."

– Robert Louis Stevenson

During my personal training I have faced various barriers and, like many other people when attempting to make body shape changes, I have found that the closer to the goal I get, the harder it becomes. This is not just because of frustration, but because of the body's own resistance to the process of change.

Why do I mention this?

Well, it's usually at this stage that some choose to reach for medical supplements to assist/support them over the last hurdle. There's nothing necessarily wrong with this, but my attitude to this approach, and the question I always ask myself is, what happens when I stop?

Tablets are not the solution to stress or associated illnesses ... but education is.

Masking the root cause of the issue with medication and being sent on your way is not going to provide the optimum solution, and it's not the answer in terms of stress-free living – for life! Asking yourself, "What happens when I stop?" is a great tool to use within stress management and indeed in many other fields, not least within the weight loss or dieting arena. Living on supported medication or "shakes" may be all well and good for the temporary period of time in which you are benefiting from the chemicals, but what happens when you reach your goal and remove them?

The answer is simple.

Your body reverts back to the original "habits" and behaviours, but not only that, it now lacks the support of your body's own production of chemicals due to the imbalance created by those supplied from artificial sources.

"Fitness – if it came in a bottle, everybody would have a great body."

Cher

What all of this means is that stress can be *masked* with superfast-acting medication, but this fails to address the root cause of stress or answer the question of why it's in your life in the first place. The more stress is masked in this way the more likely it is that the question of why you "do" stress will remain unaddressed. One of my mantras has always been – and will remain so – *the more you avoid something, the more you will face it on your journey.*

We have become a masking society rather than a resolution society.

Drugs

I always ask my clients if they are taking any drugs or anti-depressants and, if they are, I'm keen for them to be able to reduce the amount they take or come off them completely throughout the course of their sessions. However, I must make it clear that I have the utmost respect for the medical profession and my reason for wanting to reduce medication is simply that I believe modern medicine is flawed. This is through no fault of the professionals or the people on the ground but, as I see it, it's essentially the fault of our culture and the influences of the media. We live in a "quick fix" society and this creates time pressures – medical professionals simply do not have the time to address the root cause.

There is very little to stop someone who is perfectly well creating the impression that they have an "illness" and being prescribed a wonder pill to mask the issues. Obviously, this is unlikely to be the case when someone clearly has an injury or other physical issue, but in the case of mental issues, things are not always so clear and this is when time pressures lead to the prescription of a "pill" rather than an investigation into the root cause.

Medication is not the answer to eradication.

Weight issues provide a good example. Someone with weight issues will always return to their prior state after a diet, and this is simply because they have not addressed the original issues or answered the question of why they became overweight in the first instance. Exactly the same can be applied to stress. Unless the original cause is addressed, any action you take will simply mask it until a pressure/stressor is applied with enough force to generate a relapse.

You are the architect of your own body and mind; create something that will provide you with a lifetime of stress free living.

Now is a good time to revisit the proven mental as well as physical health benefits of exercise and to plan how you will make the best use of your dedicated time for exercise. If you're new to exercise, begin by visiting your local GP for a general health check and to get the "all clear" to go ahead. In the same way that a car must go through a Ministry of Transportation test (MOT) each year to ensure it remains roadworthy, your body also needs a regular MOT to make sure there's no evidence of potentially hazardous wear and tear. A bit of rust in your car's bodywork doesn't cause it to fail an MOT but small problem areas that are likely to become bigger problems if left unchecked need to be given appropriate attention – and so it is with your body. Mechanics designed for movement seize up when left stationary for long periods – and so it is with your body! There's an expression, "If you don't use it, you lose it", which in relation to your body simply means that if you don't use your ability to move, you lose your ability to move.

In the same way that *thinking* you can't cook blinkers you to a world of home-cooked meals that are simple to prepare as well as simply delicious, *thinking* you don't have any interest in exercise or any inclination to try it blinkers you to a world of feeling physically and mentally better. Getting into an exercise habit is easier than you think. It takes very little time to begin realizing the benefits of exercise, and when you experience the feel-good factor it generates, you have all the motivation you need to continue.

Take a walk ...

A simple and motivational way to get into regular exercise is to try a walking exercise based on an idea devised originally by the Merrell footwear company in the US. Their version is known as the Merrell® 10-minute Challenge but my abbreviated version is simply the Bonetti Walk Challenge. All you need is a comfy pair of shoes, a walking route that measures 800 metres (half a mile) and a watch to time how long it takes you to walk the distance.

Simply walk the route – at no more than a moderate level of intensity – and compare the time it takes you to complete the distance to the times on the chart that follows.

The Bonetti Walk Challenge

Time chart for **women** (times given are in minutes and seconds):

Age	under 30	under 40	under 50	50+
Great	less than 5.30	less than 6.00	less than 6.30	less than 7.00
Good	less than 6.30	less than 7.00	less than 7.30	less than 8.00
Average	7.30	8.00	8.30	9.00
Not so good	up to 9.00	up to 10.00	up to 10.30	up to 11.00
Really not good	over 9.00	over 10.00	over 10.30	over 11.00

Time chart for **men:**

Great	under 5.15	under 5.30	under 5.45	under 6.00
Good	under 6.15	under 6.30	under 6.45	under 7.00
Average	7.15	7.30	7.45	8.00
Not so good	up to 8.30	up to 9.00	up to 9.15	up to 9.45
Really not good	over 8.30	over 9.00	over 9.15	over 9.45

Whatever time it takes you to complete the distance, make it your aim to either improve on it or maintain it by committing to walking regularly.

Remember, if you don't use it, you lose it.

There's a saying, "The best form of exercise for you is any exercise you'll do" and these are wise words. It's not important *how* you exercise, it's only important that you do and that you continue to do it regularly. It goes without saying that the more you enjoy taking part in an activity, the more motivated you're going to be to continue taking part. Think outside of the box and try out lots of different activities … if you don't like walking, don't give up, just try something else. The more you stimulate your body and your mind by challenging yourself to learn new things, the greater the rewards in terms of physical and mental health. Any form of exercise is better than no exercise at all but a team of researchers from Exeter and Brunel Universities are keen to promote the message that more is better. In 2007, the team head Dr Gary O'Donovan said, *"It's extremely worrying that British adults now believe that a brief stroll and a bit of gardening is enough to make them fit and healthy. Brisk walking offers some health benefits, but jogging, running and other vigorous activities offer maximal protection from disease."*

If you've heard of the "runner's high" experienced by not only runners but also participants in many other cardiovascular forms of exercise, you may be interested to know that scientists have now proven that it is a very real state. Exercise *does* create an endorphin-driven emotional state, which generates a very real feel-good factor.

The stress – heart disease connection

As yet, science does not have all the answers in terms of understanding the full effects of psychological stress and its impact on heart disease. However, it is known that the effects of stress on the heart influence the activities of the automatic nervous system, and this can have a negative impact in many ways, including the following:

- **A rise in blood pressure** – an immediate response to stress is an elevated heart rate, which causes the arteries to constrict and narrow, and blood pressure rises as a result.

- **Altered heart rhythms** – heart arrhythmias (abnormalities in rhythm) are known to occur as a result of emotional stress. This can be a serious concern for anyone with existing heart rhythm issues.

- **Stickier blood** – certain cells in the blood become stickier in response to stress and it's thought this is a preparatory measure taken by the body in case of an injury occurring when "fighting or fleeing" the imminent danger.

- **Build-up of fat molecules** – it's now known that the normal clearing process of fat molecules from the body is impaired by stress.

- **A thickening of the arteries** – a link has now been found between the blood vessel disease identified by a thickening of the arteries and the type of stress that often leads to depression.

- **Blood vessel damage** – according to some studies, there is evidence to suggest that sudden spikes in blood pressure experienced regularly as a result of psychological stress can lead to damage in the lining of blood vessels.

- **Inflammation** – it's now known that the body releases inflammatory markers into the bloodstream as a result of stress. The presence of these markers increases the potential risk of suffering a heart attack or stroke.

Research into the connection between stress and heart disease is ongoing but stress cardiomyopathy is a condition that is now widely recognized. In a nutshell, the condition creates symptoms such as chest pain. Chest pain can then appear to be a heart attack when monitored on an echocardiogram, but further investigation shows no evidence of any coronary artery disease or any other obstructions. This form of heart dysfunction is the result of psychological stress and, although severe, the symptoms can be reversed when appropriate stress management measures are taken.

Currently, the links between stress and heart disease are stronger in men than in women, and this is especially evident in work situations where men feel they have a lack of control. It's thought that the link may be weaker in women simply because women, on the whole, find more heart-protective ways of coping with stress compared to men. For example, choosing a relaxing bath or a walk (and talk) with friends over drinking alcohol and keeping everything bottled up inside.

Research has also shown that psychological stress may cause symptoms of acute coronary syndrome, which indicates a heart attack or an imminent heart attack. The changes in the blood brought on by stress are potentially harmful and the risks are greater in the aftermath of a stressful event than they are during it.

Now cast your mind back to the proven physical benefits of exercise discussed earlier, and two points in particular ...

A lowered risk of developing heart disease and/or suffering a stroke: current statistics show that those living an inactive lifestyle can reduce their potential of developing life-threatening heart disease by half simply by making exercise a regular part of their day.

Lower blood pressure if high: if you currently have high blood pressure, regular exercise can help to lower it, thereby reducing your risk of suffering a heart attack or stroke. Exercise can also help to prevent high blood pressure from developing in the first place.

Nutrition know-how

A more active lifestyle must be fuelled with a more plentiful supply of nutrients. It takes a healthy, balanced combination of carbohydrates, proteins and fats to create a healthy, balanced diet; however, there are many conflicting opinions on what constitutes a healthy balance. One of the most commonly used guides to healthy eating is promoted by the US Department of Agriculture (USDA) and known as the Food Guide Pyramid. The pyramid is divided into six food categories, beginning at the base with grains ...

Grains – a recommendation of 6–11 servings per day is given, and a serving might include pasta, bread, cereals, potatoes or any other starchy food. Whole grain varieties represent a better source of nutrition and fibre than white varieties.

Fruits and vegetables – a recommendation of 3–5 servings per day is given, with the emphasis on eating a variety of fresh produce to ensure all of the essential vitamins and minerals are sourced.

Meats and pulses – a recommendation of 2–3 servings per day is given, with this category including red meats, white meats, fish, eggs, beans, nuts and seeds, all of which provide a source of protein.

Dairy foods – a recommendation of 2–3 servings per day is given, with this category including milk, yoghurt and cheese, all of which provide a further source of protein along with calcium.

Fats – this category sits at the point of the pyramid and the daily serving recommendation is to "eat sparingly".

The foods you eat are your body's only source of fuel so it's important to get the best mix of nutrients possible to give your mind and body everything needed to support a top performance. According to USDA guidelines the optimum mix is 60 per cent carbohydrates, 30 per cent fats and 10 per cent proteins. As mentioned earlier, it's my choice to aim for a mix of 40 per cent proteins, 30 per cent carbohydrates and 30 per cent fats, highlighting the differing opinions on the subject of creating a healthy, balanced diet.

To find the best mix for you, adopt a three-pronged approach:

- Listen to the guidelines provided by the government and other official sources with an open mind; study the science with interest and work with people on the ground (personal trainers/fitness professionals, etc.)

who have successfully developed the body shape and level of fitness you aspire to have.

- Armed with this information, you can make informed decisions and choices over what works best for you. As individuals, we are all beginning from different starting points with different aspirations in mind, so there can be no one-size-fits-all solution.
- The best solution for you will be found by creating a balance across all three elements of stress management – lifestyle, fitness and nutrition.

Nutrition facts

Carbohydrates are generally split into two categories:

Simple carbohydrates (sugary foods) – these include all foods and drinks containing sugar, and also those containing fructose, glucose, lactose and maltose.

Complex carbohydrates (starchy foods) – these include all starchy foods such as pasta, bread and potatoes. Often described as "the athlete's best friend", complex carbohydrates provide the main fuel source in many sports-focused diets.

Fat

Contrary to the messages sent out by glossy magazines and so-called "celebrity" dieters, not all fats are "bad" and we *need* fat as part of a healthy, balanced diet. Vitamins A, D, K, E and other fat-soluble vitamins are carried around the body by fat, and it provides essential protection and insulation for the body's vital organs.

Fats can be split into three categories:

Monounsaturated fats – these are "good" fats, known to help reduce LDL cholesterol and increase HDL cholesterol levels in the blood. Sources include oils such as olive oil, rapeseed oil or groundnut oils, and it can also be found in a variety of seeds and nuts.

Polyunsaturated fats – these are also "good" fats as they contain essential fatty acids (EFAs), which cannot be produced by the body independently. EFAs play an essential role in building, maintaining and repairing the nervous system, cardiovascular system and also the immune system. Sources include walnuts, sunflower seeds and oily fish.

When the rule of "everything in moderation" is applied, a combination of polyunsaturated and monounsaturated fats in the diet is extremely beneficial to your health.

Saturated fats – these are the "bad" fats known to have a detrimental effect on your health as they are linked to heart disease and related poor health issues. Sources include meat fat and fatty meat products (e.g., sausages), butter, cheese (soft varieties in particular) and all processed foods such as cakes, biscuits, pastries, pies and many "convenience" foods.

As a point of interest, tasty ways to increase the healthy fat content of a smoothie include:

Flax seeds (linseeds) – these provide a rich source of omega-3 essential fatty acids along with B vitamins, magnesium and manganese.

Peanut butter – this provides a good source of healthy fat (unsaturated fat) along with B vitamins, vitamin E, phosphorus, iron, copper and potassium.

Almond butter – this also provides healthy fat along with vitamin E and other antioxidants.

Protein

Protein is present in your body tissues, including your muscles, tendons, bones, arteries, skin, hair and nails. It plays an important role in tissue growth and repair and for this reason is often referred to as the body's "building blocks".

It takes a healthy mix of all of these along with essential vitamins and minerals to fuel your body. To keep your body functioning at its peak and your mind focused and alert, you need to provide it with the optimum mix, but the best mix of nutrients to fuel your body and mind is ultimately your choice, so do your own homework and ensure it's an informed one.

Hydration facts

Water is essential to all life, and the human body is in fact around two-thirds water. We need it to keep all of our bodily functions in order and to get rid of waste products, but is the much touted "drink eight glasses of water per day" the best approach to hydration?

We should aim to drink around six glasses (200 ml) of water each day to make up the recommended 1.2 litre daily intake. However, the total amount of water the human body needs to replace losses on a daily basis is around 2.5 litres. Around 0.3 litres of this is recovered by natural chemical reactions in the cells and around 1 litre is sourced from the foods we eat, so the remainder must be supplied through drinking fluids. Water is the best hydrator but a diet of fresh fruits and vegetables goes a long way towards helping your body to stay adequately hydrated.

Fruits and vegetables with a high water content may be twice as effective in terms of hydrating your body after exercise as a glass of water. The reason for this is that fruits and vegetables also offer natural sugars, mineral salts, amino acids and vitamins that the body normally loses as a result of sweating during exercise. They also represent a healthier choice when compared to most sports drinks as they are free of any artificial additives such as flavourings and colours.

Mild dehydration can lead to a dip in mood as well as energy, with results showing that dehydrated individuals are more prone to angry outbursts and have greater difficulty controlling their emotions. Dehydration is also known to have a negative effect on general levels of concentration and the ability to think clearly and quickly. Dehydration affects all people, and staying properly hydrated is just as important for those who work all day at a computer as it is for marathon runners.

Something that's extremely important to realize is that thirst alone is not the most effective indicator in terms of remaining adequately hydrated. It's now known that the human body is already around 2 per cent dehydrated before the sensation of thirst is experienced and with only a 1.5 per cent level of dehydration having negative physical and mental effects, the mind and body will already be suffering the effects before you feel thirsty.

"Water is the driving force of all nature."

Leonardo da Vinci

Laughter – it really is the best medicine!

It's a common saying that "laughter is the best medicine" but scientific research has proven that laughter is indeed an effective coping mechanism in times of acute stress. Having a laugh about things or getting things in perspective and seeing the funny side is not only helpful in terms of releasing pent-up tension, anxiety or frustration, but it can also help to reduce the levels of stress hormones circulating in your body. Scientists now believe that the feelings of "uncontrollable" and intense laughter experienced by some individuals during acutely stressful events – including a tragic death – is a coping mechanism used by the body to help the mind manage the extreme emotional pain.

TOOLS

Meditational garden

This is a great exercise that can be practised as often as you wish, and without the need for anything other than your time. Anything from 5 to 40 minutes is of benefit and can stabilize "normal" thinking.

Be aware of the myths ... meditation is not an exercise that's only of benefit to those living an "alternative" lifestyle and it is in fact widely practised around the word by people from all walks of life and without any form of social standing and culture.

Although many thousands of years old and originally used as a means of connecting with your inner self, meditation has evolved into a great tool to resolve internal conflict, reduce stress and enhance relaxation. During meditation, the aim is to create clarity of thought by sorting and eliminating any disorganized matters.

There are a number of meditations, including Tai Chi, Qi Gong, Yoga, mantra and many more of equal benefit.

However, for the purpose of this exercise we will be using Guided Meditation. Guided Meditation is simply using your own visualization to create a number of mental (internal) images to enhance a state of wellbeing. It doesn't matter if you have never meditated before, or if you think you can't – if you can now *internally picture* your front door and the colour of your car, then you have all the skills you need.

The four ingredients:

One – the first is to find a comfortable place to sit or lay. You can stand, and I have seen people successfully meditating while on the underground, but to keep the whole process as simple and enjoyable as possible, sitting or lying down is preferable.

Two – the second is focused thinking. This is the part that drives all other thoughts out of your mind, making them disappear to a place without actually taking any further intervention.

Three – the third is your breathing and your timing. If you breathe hard and fast then your body will display the effects of doing so; you should now regulate your breathing to create deeper breaths at a slower rate, thereby bringing about a more relaxed physical and mental state.

Four – the fourth is your surroundings. As mentioned previously, the surroundings don't actually matter as much as you might think; however, they magnify the depth (depending on experience) you are able to go. For example, imagine sitting on a bench at your local park with noisy road works going on just behind you, and then imagine lying on soft sand while being gently warmed by the sun ... you get the idea!

Getting into state:

The four ingredients are the key areas to consider before exploring meditation, the next step is to get into state ...

1. Start with your breathing – you can practise this now as you are reading ...
2. Control the inward breath and the outward breath. Take note of how your chest rises and falls, and how with each breath you take your muscles relax that little bit further ...
3. As you continue to breathe, bring your attention to each part of your body ...
4. Start from your feet and work your way up. Notice any tingling sensations, and how the muscles simply relax as if you have given them permission. Notice any warmth within your body and bring your attention back to your breathing ...

Greet the morning stretch

This stretch is a great way to begin your day in the positive way in which you mean to go on. It can also be done at regular intervals throughout your day to keep a check on your posture, reminding you to raise your head and open your chest to breathe freely.

1. Raise both arms in front of your body to around shoulder-height and then open your arms out to each side of your body with your wrists facing forward.
2. Raise your head slightly as you open your arms and push your chest upward and outward as you take a deep breath in.
3. Relax the stretch for a moment, allowing your head and chest to lower as you slowly exhale, but keep your arms held up at shoulder-height.
4. Repeat the stretch, aiming to increase the benefits by gently arching your back as you inhale this time.

Deep breathing

Shallow, rapid breathing is commonly experienced in times of stress. This exercise helps to slow down the breathing rate and promotes the naturally calming effect of taking slower, deeper breaths. Practising this exercise at regular intervals throughout your day is an effective way to maintain a relaxed state.

1. Slowly breathe in through your nose, aiming to take a deep breath for a count of around 10.
2. Avoid any exaggerated lifting of your chest as you breathe in and place your hand on your abdomen to focus your attention on feeling your stomach expanding instead.
3. Slowly breathe out through your nose, aiming to control the breath for a count of around 10.

4. Repeat the exercise a further five times (up to 10 in times of stress) and focus your attention on controlling your breath by taking your time and internally counting to 10 in each direction.

Centring

This is another deep breathing exercise that can help to slow your breathing rate in times of stress and also improve your ability to visualize and use mental imagery when practised regularly. Deep breathing and centring exercises increase the amount of oxygen circulating in your blood helping to boost your concentration and energy levels; slower, deeper breaths help to reduce the workload on the heart by slowing the heart rate and making each breath more efficient; focusing on deep breathing reduces feelings of anger or fear, and in general promotes a state of relaxation, which can in turn improve your sleep.

As in the deep breathing exercise previously, aim to breathe in and out slowly through your nose.

1. Place one hand on your abdomen and the other on your chest. As you inhale, feel your stomach expand as if filling with air before focusing your attention on letting the air rise upward into your chest. As your stomach expands you will feel your hand lift and as your chest expands you will feel the other hand lift. It's important

not to allow your stomach hand to drop as your chest hand lifts so that the deep inhalation fills both areas. This will take a little practise.

2. When both hands have lifted, slowly exhale, feeling both hands drop as you do so.

3. Now inhale and hold your breath momentarily (or a count of one) before exhaling for a count of three.

4. Next, try inhaling and holding your breath for a count of two before exhaling for a count of five, followed by inhaling and holding for a count of three before exhaling for a count of seven.

5. With regular practice, you become able to focus entirely on your breathing and being able to follow the pattern of your breaths in this way creates a sense of deep mental relaxation.

6. Once relaxed, begin focusing on individual areas of your body to create an overall sense of physical as well as mental relaxation. Begin at the top of your head and use mental imagery to allow any muscular tension to ease. Depending on the climate where you live, you might choose to imagine the sun gently warming each area of your body as you allow the muscles to relax, or you may choose to imagine a gentle breeze cooling each area. Work your way down through each area of your head – forehead, eyelids, lips, chin and jaw – before moving on to your neck and shoulders, and then along the length of each of your arms individually to your fingertips, feeling each individual area along the way. Continue from your upper back to chest, abdomen, stomach and lower back, before focusing on your hips and each individual area down one leg followed by

the other before reaching your toes and feeling totally relaxed all the way down to the soles of your feet.

7. Enjoy the sensation of deep relaxation for as many minutes as you have available and then return your attention to your breathing, following each breath for a count of five before opening your eyes to continue your day feeling relaxed, refreshed and ready for whatever comes your way.

SUMMARY

Stress management and lifestyle change is a combination of addressing three key elements:

1. **Lifestyle** – coping with stress is not an option; it's a choice.
2. **Fitness** – science has proven that an active lifestyle brings with it many physical and mental health benefits.
3. **Nutrition** – you are what you eat so if you want to be happy, relaxed and able to enjoy life to the full, you need to provide your mind and body with the nutrients it needs for optimum health and vitality.

Miss out on any of these areas and your success will simply not be as fruitful. Your aim is not to change the cause and effects but to analyse your whole life and to make changes that will complement all aspects of it. When you get your mind to work in your favour, you get to reap the rewards of living a life in control of stress, if not totally free of stress.

Using the correct diet will further enhance your ability to deal with and overcome stress in the best way possible, but remember, your stress-free living lifestyle will be as good as you make it.

Tips to remember:

- **Eat complementary wholefoods** – these wholefoods include, but are not restricted to: whole grains, beans, nuts, seeds, fruits and root vegetables such as yam and sweet potato.
- Remember the saying, **"fresh is best"**!
- **Eat 10 a day** – eat a wide variety of vegetables and fruits (fresh is best) but keep in mind that fruits contain fructose and unless consumed in moderation, they will increase the amount of sugar held within the body. Make up the bulk of your 10 a day with a variety of vegetables. Dark leafy greens are best, and use berries as a fruit portion when available. Consider mixing up some "green smoothies" for a wild variety of flavours!
- **Eat more often** – the principle behind eating smaller meals spread across the day is to provide your body with a steady flow of nutrients. This is something I learned to use to good effect within the fitness arena but it is equally effective when managing stress or improving mental abilities. Eating six or so smaller meals rather than three larger meals helps to speed up your metabolism and keep your mind fresh with a constant supply of essential nutrients.
- *Enjoy* your food – take time out to eat in a relaxed environment. Avoid eating "on the move" and give yourself time to enjoy your food as well as giving your body the best chance of fully digesting and absorbing the vitamins and minerals it needs.
- **Make good choices** – eating healthily is not just a matter of the amount of food you eat; it's also a matter

of making good food choices. It goes without saying that foods that have remained close to their natural state represent better choices than foods that have been highly processed. However, while fresh is generally best and will normally offer a higher nutritional value than tinned or frozen versions, there can be times when "fresh produce" is no longer as fresh as it could be after spending lengthy periods of time on display. When this is the case, frozen fruits and vegetables – especially the "frozen at source" varieties – may in fact represent the better choice.

- **Healthy choices?** – avoid the trap of thinking "organic" represents "healthy" because, while organically grown produce may represent a more natural choice, a Victoria sponge cake made with organic flour, filled with organic raspberry jam and dusted with organically grown sugar is not a "healthy" cake!

- **Read the labels** – the above also applies to "low fat" products. Don't let the word "light" on the packaging lead you into believing it's a healthier option. It may contain less fat than a "full fat" version of the same but there's every chance that it contains more sugar or salt or other undesirable ingredient to make up the difference. Take the time to read the labels.

- **Every little helps** – and remember, it takes a commitment of only 10 minutes each day to begin developing an "exercise habit" and the benefits you feel almost instantly will very quickly provide you with all the motivation you need to continue. It's not about finding extra time for regular exercise, it's about making better use of the time you have.

"Stress is like spice – in the right proportion it enhances the flavor of a dish. Too little produces a bland, dull meal; too much may choke you"

Donald Tubesing

Remember, the amount of stress you "do" in your life is your choice. Do you want to continue feeling anxious; finding it hard to relax or take time out; struggling to rid that constant mental ache, and *suffering* from stress? Or, do you want to become free of stress and free to live a life of clarity as a result?

It's your choice to make. Make it NOW.

Some final stats on stress to help you make that choice right now ...

A survey focused on revealing the impact of stress on everyday life found the following:

54 per cent of those surveyed reported that stress had led to fights with family members and close friends.

48 per cent felt stress had a negative impact on both their personal life and their working life.

35 per cent felt work pressures and demands interfered with family and home life resulting in feelings of stress.

31 per cent of those in employment expressed feelings of stress surrounding difficulties managing both work and home life.

26 per cent expressed feelings of being alienated from family and friends as a result of stress.

Don't be a statistic; stress less and be happy.

"You're only here for a short visit. Don't hurry, don't worry. And be sure to smell the flowers along the way."

Walter Hagen

ABOUT BENJAMIN BONETTI

Benjamin Bonetti is considered one of the leading authorities within the self-help arena and has produced several leading hypnosis products.

Bonetti promotes and writes about the power of positive thinking and the essential need to take massive action. He is known to talk about his early struggles and refers to them in several of his early written pieces as the building blocks to his success.

Over the last 10 years his therapy techniques and bullish tactics have attracted many critics who believe that the no-nonsense approach can be interpreted as too forceful, especially to those with more sensitive issues. Bonetti, however, believes that it is this technique that is often overlooked by more "fluffy" type therapies and the reason behind relapses.

Bonetti started his career in the British Army, serving for several years until later pursuing his dream of owning his own business; his entrepreneurial spirit has led him to own several businesses and later establish Benjamin Bonetti Ltd.

Bonetti has several well-known family links, and is related to Peter Bonetti (The Cat), the English goal keeper whose successful career saw him playing for both Chelsea and England during the 1970s.

Outside of business, Bonetti has been seen to promote the "voice" of the youth and during 2004 stood for local election, as the youngest person in history for that Council. Bonetti is also a keen and active conservationist, and volunteers for various countryside management organizations.

Although many of Bonetti's clients still remain unknown, he is often spotted behind the scenes at events supporting known A-list celebrities and artists. During a 2009 New Year's Day interview with the BBC Asian Network, Bonetti was referred to as a "celebrity must have secret weapon".

The success of his personal development audio recordings has led to the recordings being available internationally, including in the UK, Ireland, Mexico, the USA, Australia, New Zealand and Hong Kong.

http://www.benjaminbonetti.com

@BenjaminBonetti

Facebook: Benjamin Bonetti

Also available from Benjamin Bonetti

Books

- *How to Change Your Life*: Capstone Publishing, 2013 – ISBN 9780857084644
- *Fat Body Fat Mind*: Createspace, 2012 – ISBN 1479167355
- *Don't Struggle Quietly*: Createspace, 2012 – ISBN 1475153422
- *Inspirational & Motivational Quotes*: Createspace, 2010 – ISBN 1456333658
- *Entrepreneurs Always Drive On Empty*: Createspace, 2010 – ISBN 1453771093

Seminars & Training:

- The Law Of Attraction – The Truth
- NLP Practitioner Training UK & Overseas
- NLP Master Practitioner Training UK & Overseas
- Fat Body, Fat Mind – Coming Soon

Bonetti has produced a wide range of Hypnosis CDs and MP3s. The value of these is unknown to date, but consist of one of the largest range of hypnosis recordings by any one person.

2013 Advance Hypnotic Technique Audio CDs

- The Easy Way to Lose Weight with Hypnosis, Audiogo: 2013. ISBN 1471326284
- The Easy Way to Beat Insomnia and Sleep Easy with Hypnosis, Audiogo: 2013. ISBN 1471326322

- The Easy Way to Increase Self-Confidence with Hypnosis, Audiogo: 2013. ISBN 1471326306
- The Easy Way to Stop Smoking with Hypnosis, Audiogo: 2013. ISBN 1471326314
- The Easy Way to Become Stress Free with Hypnosis, Audiogo: 2013. ISBN 1471326292

2013 Advance Hypnotic Technique Audios MP3s

- The Easy Way to Lose Weight with Hypnosis, Audiogo: 2013. ASIN: B00ANZ392S
- The Easy Way to Increase Self-Confidence with Hypnosis, Audiogo: 2013. ASIN: B00ANZ32ZW
- The Easy Way to Stop Smoking with Hypnosis, Audiogo: 2013. ASIN: B00ANZ37DO
- The Easy Way to Beat Insomnia and Sleep Easy with Hypnosis, Audiogo: 2013. ASIN: B00ANZ38CY
- The Easy and Original Hypnotic Gastric Band, Audiogo: 2013. ASIN: B00ANZ36OY
- The Easy Way to Relax during Pregnancy, Audiogo: 2013. ASIN: B00ANZ30R2
- The Easy Way to Beat Nail Biting with Hypnosis, Audiogo: 2013. ASIN: B00ANZ31K8
- The Easy Way to Improve Self-Belief with Hypnosis, Audiogo: 2013. ASIN: B00ANZ326G
- The Easy Way to Overcome Anxiety with Hypnosis, Audiogo: 2013. ASIN: B00ANZ35EU
- The Easy Way to Become Stress Free with Hypnosis, Audiogo: 2013. ASIN: B00ANZ3036

Author photo supplied with permission of Simon Howard – http://www.snhfoto.com/

INDEX

Index

DISCARD